Phil H. LISTEMANN

ISBN: 979-1096490-53-0

© 2019 Philedition - Phil Listemann
Colour artwork: Chris Thomas
Layout & project design: Phil Listemann

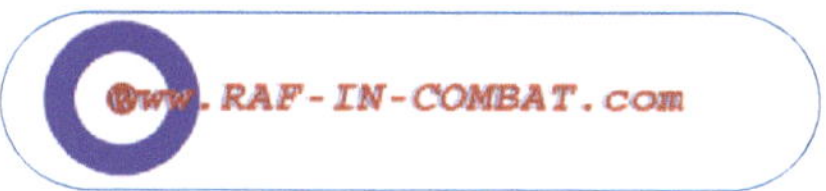

Foreword

The conduct of a successful air campaign requires a combination of strategy, tactics, capable aircraft, well trained pilots - and good leadership.

During WW2, the RAF, Commonwealth (RCAF, RAAF, RNZAF and SAAF) and 'Free European' forces employed almost 250 fighter squadrons throughout the World, from the Aleutians to the South Pacific, throughout Europe, the Middle East and North Africa, India, Burma and the East Indies and East Africa. The RAF's basic tactical formation was the squadron, and this was the first step of independent commanders usually held by a Squadron Leader. The period in command could vary from a matter of days to over a year and so many hundreds of men were appointed as Officers Commanding (OC) of a squadron. As tactics developed and larger formations were used in action, several squadrons would operate in concert and were grouped together as a Wing, led by a Wing Leader. usually of Wing Commander rank. By the mid war years as these Wings became independent mobile formations, the command was given to a Group Captain with leadership in the air held by the Wing Leader, more formally titled as Wing Commander Flying (WingCo). Most were highly decorated, and some were very successful aces but all were highly experienced with a proven record of leadership and ability.

The aim of this series is to introduce these men so far as available information allows by giving short biography and describing the operational units that they led during the war.

Acknowledgement:
André Bar, Steve Brew, Hugh Haliday, Michael Schoeman, Paul Sortehaug,
Andrew Thomas, Chris Thomas, Pavel Vancata.

The range of military decoration for airmen during the war was large, and this is not the aim here to recall of them. The Victoria Cross was the highest award, but only one fighter pilot had had the honour to receive it over the 32 Victoria Crosses awarded during WW2. However, some were regulary awarded to airmen, and specifically to the fighter leaders.

The **Victoria Cross (VC)** is Britain's highest military honour. First instituted by Queen Victoria during the Crimean War in 1856, the VC is awarded for *"most conspicuous bravery, or some daring or pre-eminent act of valour or self-sacrifice, or extreme devotion to duty in the presence of the enemy."* The bronze cross is cast from Russian guns captured at Sevastapol. In the century and a half since its creation, 1 351 have been awarded and only three bars.

The **Distinguished Service Order (DSO)**, is open to officers of all services, and was awarded from 1886 for *"distinguished services during active operations against the enemy."* From 1917 this specifically required action under fire. The order is generally given to officers in command above the rank of Flight Lieutenant/1st Lieutenant and awards to ranks below this are usually for a high degree of gallantry just short of deserving the Victoria Cross.

The **Distinguished Flying Cross** (DFC) is a military decoration awarded to personnel of the United Kingdom's Royal Air Force and other services, and formerly to officers of other Commonwealth countries, for *"an act or acts of valour, courage or devotion to duty whilst flying in active operations against the enemy"*.
The award was established on 3 June 1918, shortly after the formation of the RAF. A DFC can be awarded to a steady, rock solid, dependable pilot, or one who has shown noticeable growth and improvement over a period of time.
During the Second World War, 20,354 DFCs were awarded, the most of any award, with approximately 1,550 first bars and 45 second bars. Honorary awards were made on 964 occasions to aircrew from other non-commonwealth countries.

The **Distinguished Flying Medal** (DFM) was until 1993 a military decoration awarded to personnel of the Royal Air Force (United Kingdom) and the other services, and formerly also to personnel of other Commonwealth countries, below commissioned rank, for *"an act or acts of valour, courage or devotion to duty whilst flying in active operations against the enemy"*.
The medal was established on 3 June 1918. It was the other ranks' equivalent to the Distinguished Flying Cross, which was awarded to commissioned officers and Warrant Officers (although WOs could also be awarded the DFM), although it ranked below the DFC in order of precedence, between the Military Medal and the Air Force Medal. In 1993 the DFM was discontinued, and since then the Distinguished Flying Cross has been awarded to personnel of all ranks.
During World War II, 6,637 DFMs were awarded, with 60 first award bars and a unique second bar. Some 165 were awarded to aircrew from other non- Commonwealth countries.

List of pilots - Volume I

J.W.M. **A**ITKEN (UK)	A. **G**LOWACKI (Pol)	J.G. **M**UNRO (UK)
R.L.R **A**TCHERLEY (UK)	E.J. **G**RACIE (UK)	J.J. **O**'**M**EARA (UK)
J.P. **B**ARTLE (Aus)	C.L. **G**REEN (SR)	J. **O**RZECHOWSKI (Pol)
R.A. **B**ERG (Nor)	D.A. **G**UILLAUME (Bel)	J.M.G. **P**LAMONDON (Can)
J. **B**ERRY (UK)	K. McD. **H**AMPSHIRE (Aus)	J.R. **R**ATTEN (Aus)
K. **B**IRKSTED (Dan)	L.C.L. **H**AWKINS (UK)	B.D. **R**USSEL (Can)
N.H. **B**RETZ (Can)	G.U. **H**ILL (Can)	A.H. **S**AGER (Can)
E.T. **B**ROUGH (NZ)	J.D.W. **H**UMAN (SA)	S. **S**KALSKI (Pol)
G.A. **B**ROWN (UK)	P.A. **H**UNTER (UK)	O. **S**MIK (Cz)
A.G. **C**ONWAY (UK)	J.E. **J**OHNSON (UK)	L.E. **S**MITH (UK)
J. **C**UNNINGHAM (UK)	O.C. **K**ALLIO (USA)	R.N.B. **S**TEVENS (Aus)
J-F. **D**EMOZAY (Fr)	M.W.B. **K**NIGHT (NZ)	W.W. **S**TRAIGHT (UK)
J.S. **D**EWAR (UK)	K.C. **K**UHLMANN (SA)	F. **T**HORSAGER (Nor)
A.E.R. **E**SAU (Aus)	B.J.E. **L**ANE (UK)	A.E. **U**MBERS (NZ)
A. **E**YRE (UK)	G.J. **L**E **M**ESURIER (SA)	B. **VAN DER** **S**TOCK (NL)
B.E.F. **F**INUCANE (Ire)	D.A.R. **L**E **R**OY **DU** **V**IVIER	T. **V**YBIRAL (Cz)
J.E. **F**ROST (SA)	(Bel)	G.B. **W**ARNES (UK)
I.R. **G**LEED (UK)	E.D. **M**ACKIE (NZ)	

Squadron Leader
pennant

Wing Commander
pennant
(WingCo flying)

Group Captain
pennant
(OC Wing - Non flying or Station commander)

AITKEN,
**John William Maxwell,
RAF**

AAF No. 91028

British

DSO, DFC

Born in Montreal, Quebec, 'Max' Aitken, was educated in Great Britain. In 1935 he joined
No. 601 (County of London) Squadron. When the squadron was mobilised, in September 1939, it was flying the
fighter version of the Blenheim. In February 1940 the squadron re-equipped with Hurricanes and, in May-June
1940, saw considerable action over Belgium and France. Aitken made his first claims on 18 May. He was appointed
OC of the squadron at the end of June and was awarded the DFC in July. His command was short, however, as he
left the unit before the month was out and was assigned to non-operational duties for a couple of months. He returned to operations in February 1941 as OC of **No. 68 Squadron**. He would lead the night fighter unit until February
1943, flying Beaufighters, and made a dozen claims. In August 1942 he was awarded the DSO for his actions as CO. He
was then posted to the Eastern Mediterranean as a Group Captain but still managed to fly from time to time on operations. During one such flight, in March 1944, he made his final claims while flying a Beaufighter of No. 46 Squadron
and ended the war with a total of 15 confirmed victories (one shared), one probable and three damaged.
Returning to the UK, he eventually took command of Coastal Command's Mosquito Strike Wing at Banff during the last
months of the war.

A Beaufighter Mk.IF of No. 68 Sqn. Under
Aitken's command, the unit, which included
a Czech flight, claimed more than 25
confirmed and probable victories.

ATCHERLEY,
Richard Llewelyn Roger, RAF

RAF No. 16140

British

-

'Batchy' Atcherley enlisted in the RAF in 1922. Two years later he was flying as a fighter pilot with No. 29 Squadron at Duxford. He subsequently served with No. 23 Squadron at Kenley and No. 14 Squadron in the Middle East. There followed, from 1934, various staff positions before he was posted as OC **No. 219 Squadron** in October 1939 which was being re-formed on Blenheim Mk.IFs. He put the squadron on operational status in February 1940 and relinquished command the following May. He was then appointed OC of Air Element BEF in Norway and, after the evacuation from Norway, became OC of RAF Drem. Other staff positions followed over the next two years, commanding No. 54 OTU, RAF Fairwood Common and RAF Kenley in 1942 where he continued to fly the occasional operation and was even shot down by Fw190s on 26 May, 1942. Fortunately, he was rescued in the Channel. He was appointed to various staff positions afterwards, in the Middle East and in the UK, and ended the war as a Group Captain. Continuing to serve with the RAF after the war he eventually reached the rank of Air-Marshal before retiring in 1956.

The Spitfire Mk.VB BM316, carrying his initials, used by Richard Atcherley while OC RAF Kenley in 1942. He flew a couple of missions with this aircraft but was obliged to stop under orders from HQ. He was shot down in another Spitfire, BM235, on 26 May 1942.

From Western Australia, 'Jack' Bartle enlisted in the RAAF in September 1940. Trained in Australia, he was sent, the next year, to the Middle East and was posted to No. 112 Squadron in September 1941 to fly Curtiss Tomahawks. Two months later, on 22 November, he made his first claim against a Bf109. In June 1942, when he left the squadron, his score had risen to seven confirmed victories (one shared), one probable and two claimed as damaged (the number of confirmed victories varies from four to seven) and he was a Flight commander. He was then posted as OC of No. 1 Air Ambulance Unit flying DH86s.

Returning to operations in March 1943, he took command of **No. 450 (RAAF) Squadron**. He led this unit on fighter-bomber sorties over Tunisia, Sicily and Italy until the end of his tour in November 1943. While making no more claims, he was awarded the DFC in January 1944. He did not return to operations before he was discharged from the RAAF in July 1945.

The Curtiss Kittyhawk was the standard RAF fighter-bomber from 1942 until the end of the war and served in the Western Desert, Tunisia, Sicily and Italy. The Mk.III was the mark most used by early 1943. Here, some 450 Squadron's Mk.III at Kairouan (Tunisia) in April 1943. No. 450 Sqn only served in the Mediterranean and claimed 52 confirmed and probable victories during WW2.

Rolf Berg was an NCO in the Norwegian Army Air Service when the Germans invaded Norway. In June 1940 he sailed with the British evacuating the country and was re-trained and posted to No. 43 Squadron in July 1941 as a Second Lieutenant. He was posted to the recently formed **No. 331 (Norwegian) Squadron** two months later and made his first claim against the Luftwaffe the following May (a shared damaged Bf109). He claimed his first confirmed enemy aircraft three months later during Operation 'Jubilee' over Dieppe. He left the squadron in January on completion of his tour having become a flight commander in the meantime. In May 1943, shortly after having been awarded the DFC, Berg returned to 331 to take command of the squadron. He continued to make claims before relinquishing command in October. He returned to operations, after a couple of months' rest, to become WingCo flying of **No. 132 (Norwegian) Wing** in March 1944 (now under 2nd TAF authority). He led the Wing until his death, on 3 February 1945, when he was shot down by flak in PV181 while undertaking a low level attack on a German airfield in Holland. A month before he had received a Bar to his DFC. A well-deserved DSO was awarded posthumously. He is credited with six confirmed victories, two probables and three shared damaged.

Spitfire BM579/FN-B of 331 Squadron was regularly flown by Lt Rolf Berg in the summer of 1942.
(A. Thomas)

**Supermarine Spitfire Mk IX PV181, Lt-Col R.A. Berg,
No. 132 Wing, B.60 Grimbergen, Belgium, January 1945**

**Supermarine Spitfire Mk IX PV181, Lt-Col R.A. Berg,
No. 132 Wing, B.79 Woensdrecht, Holland, January 1945**

BERRY,
Joseph,
RAF

RAF No. 118435

British

DFC & Two Bars

'Joe' Berry joined the RAF in August 1940 and started his operational career one year later as an NCO pilot with No. 256 Squadron flying Defiants on night fighter operations. Commissioned in March 1942, he later served with Nos. 153 and 255 Squadrons in North Africa and Italy, flying Beaufighters, where he made his first claim, on 9 September 1943, followed by two others in quick succession. He returned to the UK in December and, for his actions with 255, was awarded the DFC in March 1944. In the meantime, he had joined the Fighter Interception Unit (a unit formed to develop night interception techniques). During the summer of 1944, with the new V-1 threat, a flight of Tempests was added to the unit and Berry soon distinguished himself by shooting down more than 50 V-1s in two months. The Tempest Flight of the FIU was absorbed into **No. 501 (County of Gloucester) Squadron** in August and Berry became the CO. He continued to hunt the V-1s with success and received a Bar to his DFC in September. In October, with the threat of the V-1s diminishing, 501 returned to the offensive and carried out many 'Ranger' sorties. It was during one such Ranger mission on 2 October that Berry was hit by ground fire and killed in the subsequent crash (Tempest EJ600/SD-F). At the time, he had shot down 60 V-1s, one being shared, and was, consequently, the top-scorer against the 'Doodlebug'. A second Bar to his DFC was awarded the day before his death and gazetted on 12 February, 1946.

Three Hawker Tempests of No. 501 Sqn flying in formation, during the summer of 1944, at the height of the V-1 hunt. Berry was the top scorer against the V-1s. No. 501 was credited with more than 200 aircraft destroyed and probably destroyed during the war (and at least 84 V-1s, maybe over 100).

BIRKSTED,
Kaj,
RNAF

N. 1154

Dane

DSO, DFC

Kaj Birksted was one of the few Danes who served with the RAF during the war. He was already an officer in the Danish Naval Air Service when his country was invaded by the Germans in April 1940. He fled to Sweden and then to Norway with the aim of joining the British forces fighting in this country. When the British evacuated Norway, he was evacuated with them. After completing his training he was posted to No. 43 Squadron at the end of June 1941 but was sent to the newly established **No. 331 (Norwegian) Squadron** just one month later as a Flight commander. He claimed his first victory one year later on 19 June. He was appointed OC of the squadron in August and decorated with a DFC the following month. He led 331 until the end of his first tour in April 1943.

He started another tour at the end of July 1943, as WingCo flying of **No. 132 (Norwegian) Airfield** (Wing in May 1944) as a Lieutenant-Colonel of the RNoAF, and continued to enjoy considerable success as he claimed roughly half of his claims as a Wing leader. For his action he was awarded the DSO in November 1943. He claimed his last victory on 23 January 1944 and left the Wing two months later at the end of his tour. He returned to operations in March 1945 for a third tour and flew Mustangs as WingCo flying of the **Bentwaters Wing**.

He survived the war with 11 confirmed victories (one shared) and three damaged. He later served with the post-war Danish Air Force.

Spitfire Mk.IX MH830, coded 'KB', with which Kaj Birksted made his last claim on 23 January 1944.

Supermarine Spitfire Mk IX BS458, Lt-Col K. Birksted, No. 132 Airfield, North Weald, United Kingdom, August-October 1943

BRETZ,
Norman Hobson,
RCAF

CAN./ J.2975

Canadian

DFC

'Norm' Bretz, from Toronto, enlisted in the RCAF in April 1940 and undertook his training in Canada. By the end of the year he had received his wings and his commission and was then sent overseas. He was first posted, in December, to No. 2 Squadron RCAF, based in Britain, which was converting from Army Co-operation work to fighter duties. In March 1941 the squadron was re-numbered **No. 402 (RCAF) Squadron** . In 1941 the squadron was engaged in fighter-bomber missions with its Hurricanes. By early 1942 Bretz had been promoted to Flight Lieutenant and took charge of B Flight. In mid-August 1942 he was given command of the squadron which was now flying the recently introduced Spitfire Mk.IX. That month was one not to forget for Bretz as he made his first claims with one confirmed destroyed Fw190 and two aircraft damaged (including one during Operation 'Jubilee' over Dieppe on the 19th). The next month he added another aircraft damaged to his credit. This was his last claim. He left 402 at the end of September, with a DFC just gazetted, to take command of **No. 411 (RCAF) Squadron**. 'Norm' Bretz ended his tour in March 1943. At the end of 1943 he returned to operational duties by becoming the WingCo flying of the **Digby Wing**. He remained at the head of the Wing until April 1944 when it was transferred to the 2nd TAF. He was repatriated and did not return to operations before the end of the war.

When Norm Bretz became the CO of No. 402 Sqn, BS430 became his regular aircraft. Note the red Maple Leaf on the white disc. This began to appear in 1942. No.402 claimed more than 50 aircraft destroyed and probably destroyed during the war.

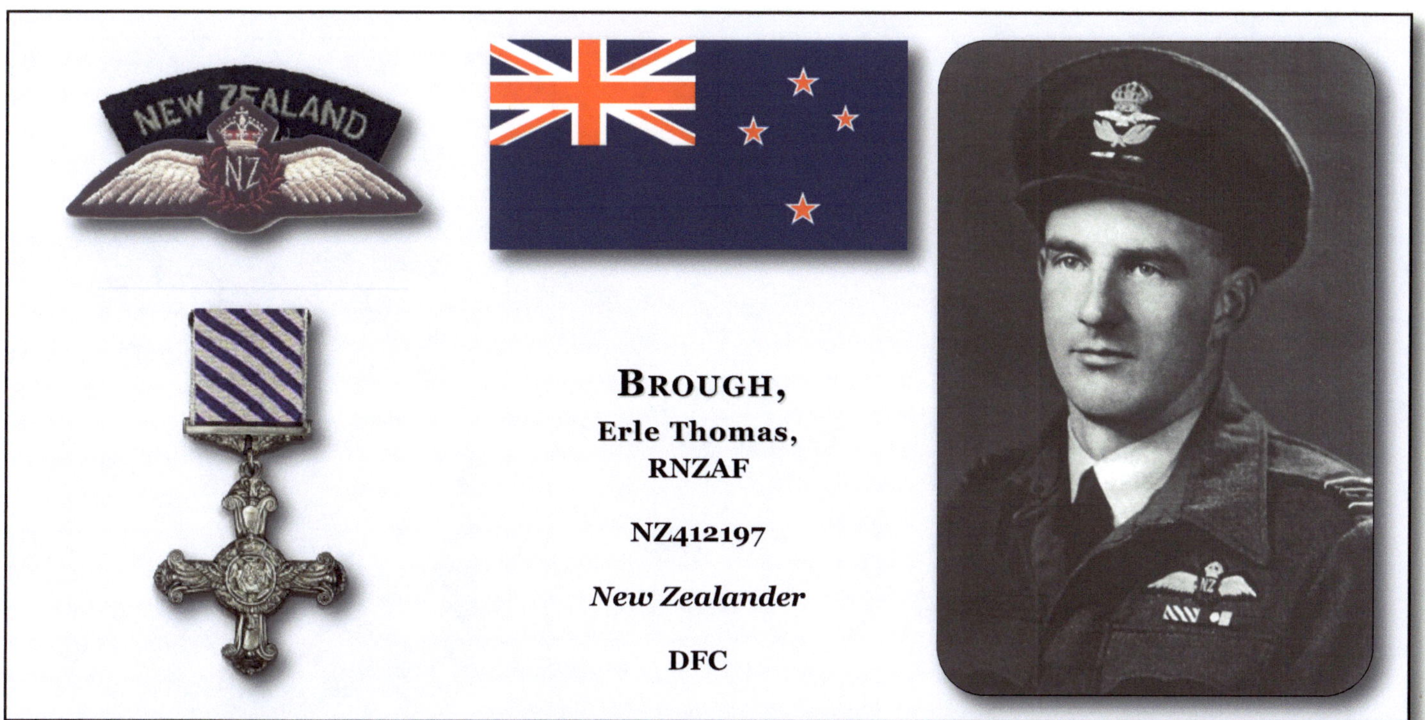

BROUGH,
Erle Thomas,
RNZAF

NZ412197

New Zealander

DFC

Erle Brough joined the RNZAF in April 1941. He undertook his initial training in New Zealand and sailed to the UK at the end of 1941 as an NCO. Once his OTU course was completed in Britain he was posted to No. 132 (Bombay) Squadron in April 1942 to fly Spitfires. A few weeks later he was in Malta flying with No. 603 (City of Edinburgh) Squadron before being posted to No. 229 Squadron in August where he made his first claims. In November that year he returned to Britain, later commissioned, and served as a flying instructor at No. 59 OTU. In August 1943 he started a second tour of operations on Typhoons with No. 182 Squadron. He became a Flight commander the following March. In September he was promoted to Squadron Leader and took command of **No. 137 Squadron**. This was just after he had claimed an Fw190 as probably destroyed (his only claim in Western Europe) which brought his total to two confirmed victories (one shared) one probable and one aircraft damaged. He received a DFC in September 1944 for his actions with No. 182 Squadron. He left 137 at Eindhoven a few days before Christmas 1944 and returned home to New Zealand. He did not see any more action after that and left the RNZAF in June 1945.

A Typhoon of No. 137 Sqn, MN627/SF-N, under maintenance at the end of the summer 1944. This unit was one of the first to use rockets against ground targets and was credited with five confirmed and probable victories and 30 V-1s destroyed.

BROWN,
George Alfred,
RAF

RAF No. 39851

British

DFC

George Brown joined the RAF on a short service commission in April 1937. At the outbreak of the war he was serving with No. 66 Squadron with which he would make his two claims, one confirmed Ju87 and another unconfirmed over Rotterdam on 13 May. Soon after, he was posted to No. 253 Squadron and participated in the Battle of Britain until being wounded in action on 30 August.

He recovered from his injuries and was posted to the newly formed No. 71 (Eagle) Squadron - the first American-manned fighter unit - as a Flight commander. He remained with 71 until August 1941 when he was chosen to lead the third and last 'Eagle' squadron, **No. 133 (Eagle) Squadron**, then under formation and to bring the new pilots up to operational standard. He left the unit in November for a staff appointment at HQ Fighter Command and was awarded the DFC the following month. For his second tour of operations he was given command of **No. 257 (Burma) Squadron**, flying Typhoons, and led the unit until the end of his tour in April 1943. No more operational postings followed and he served in the Middle East until the end of war where he could be found commanding RAF Nicosia. He continued his career in the RAF after the war and retired as a Group Captain in July 1962.

Flight Lieutenant George A. Brown's personal mount, Hawker Hurricane Mk.IIB Z3781, while he was 'A' Flight Commander of No. 71 (Eagle) Squadron at North Weald during the summer 1941. In two years, until September 1942 when the squadron was disbanded, No.71 claimed 53.5 aircraft destroyed or probably destroyed.

Arthur Conway enlisted in the RAF at the age of 17, in 1940, by lying about his birth date. One year later, in October 1941, he was posted to No. 136 Squadron and left for the Middle East the following month. The squadron was diverted to the Far East to try to stop the Japanese offensive in the region. Flying Hurricanes, he saw action over Burma, and claimed three Japanese fighters destroyed and one more damaged in the spring of 1943. For his long service with 136, he was awarded the DFC in November 1943. The following month the squadron converted to the Spitfire Mk.V and returned to operations with Conway now a Flight commander. With the Spitfire, Conway soon showed his skills and in the following weeks claimed four aircraft destroyed, one more probable and three damaged. His tour ended in March 1944 and he returned to operations in May 1945 as OC of **No. 155 Squadron**, a posting he left in November. He remained in the RAF after the war.

Spitfire Mk.VIII MV483 became Conway's personal mount in the summer of 1945 and he carried out a couple of ground support sorties with this aircraft. The chance of meeting any Japanese aircraft was slim and Conway did not add to his tally while at the head of No. 155 Sqn. This unit fought for the entire war in the Far East and its pilots claimed about 25 confirmed and probable victories.

CUNNINGHAM,
John,
RAF

AAF **No. 90216**

British

DSO & Two Bars, DFC & Bar

John Cunningham joined the Auxiliary Air Force in 1935 and flew with
No. 604 (County of Middlesex) Squadron. He started the war with this unit, being called up for permanent duty just
before the war broke out. The squadron was flying the Blenheim Mk.IF on day and night operations. One year later, 604
received its first Beaufighter Mk.Is and switched to night operations exclusively. Cunningham claimed his first victory on the
night of 19/20 November and, in January 1941, was awarded the DFC. Thereafter, successes mounted rapidly and included
three victories in a single night (15/16 April 1941) which earned him the DSO. In June, his tally had risen to 13 confirmed
victories but, as the Luftwaffe had almost deserted the British skies for the Eastern front, the regularity of claims slowed. He
took command of the squadron in August and a Bar to his DFC followed in September. He relinquished command of 604 in
July 1942 for a well-deserved rest after adding one confirmed victory and one aircraft damaged in 1942 and a Bar to his DSO.
Returning to operations in January 1943 as OC **No. 85 Squadron**. He led the unit until March 1944 and earned a second
Bar to his DSO and made a couple of more claims. Promoted to Group Captain, he did not see any more operational postings
before the end of war. He ended the war with 20 confirmed victories, three probables and seven more damaged.

A No. 604 Sqn Beaufighter, the
type in which Cunningham made
most of his claims. His successes
had to be shared with his radar
operator, C.F. 'Jimmy' Rawsley
who was awarded a DSO, a DFC
and a DFM & Bar. No. 604 was
credited with about 175 victories,
confirmed or probable.

DEMOZAY,

Jean-François

Alias 'MORLAIX',
FFAF

F. 30581

French

DSO, DFC & Bar

Demozay, like many young French men, was called up for military service in 1938 but invalided two weeks later for health reasons before being finally accepted for non-combatant duties in September 1939. His knowledge of the English language led him to become an interpreter attached to the RAF. He was seconded to No. 1 Squadron. Unable to leave the country while France was collapsing, and his unit withdrawing to England, he chose to flee and, using his basic flight skills, flew to the UK in an abandoned Bristol Bombay with 15 men aboard. Before the month was over, he joined the Free French Air Force and took the name of *Morlaix*. In August he was sent to No. 5 OTU to complete his training as a fighter pilot. He joined No. 1 Squadron in October and made his first claim on 8 November when he damaged a Ju88. In June 1941, with more claims on his credit, he was posted to No. 242 (Canadian) Squadron with which he made more claims before being posted to **No. 91 (Nigeria) Squadron** the following month as a Flight commander. He was awarded the DFC in October. When he left the squadron, in January at the end of his tour, he was among the top three fighter aces of 1941. In June 1942 he returned to the squadron as OC. He handed over command in December with a Bar to his DFC and a DSO. He made more claims during his command with the last, on 31 October, bringing his total to 18 confirmed, two probables and four damaged. Promoted to Wing Commander, Demozay spent the rest of the war in various non-operational positions. He was killed shortly after the end of war in a flying accident, on 19 December, when the aircraft in which he was a passenger crashed on landing at Buc.

A Spitfire Mk.V of No. 91 Sqn in 1942. The Mk.V was the principle fighter of Fighter Command at the time. No. 91, which only flew Spitfires, had a couple of 'firsts' as it was the first unit to fly the Mk.XII and the F.21 on operations. The squadron was credited with more than 100 confirmed and probable victories during the war.

DEWAR,
John Scatliff,
RAF

RAF No. 26029

British

DSO, DFC

John Dewar entered the RAF in 1926 as a regular officer. After various postings as an Army Co-operation pilot, he was promoted to Squadron Leader in December 1938. When war broke out he was in a non-flying position at Thorney Island. Two months later, in November, he arrived at No. 11 Group Pool to attend a refresher course as a fighter pilot. He was posted to France in December and took command of **No. 87 Squadron**. Despite a broken shoulder, sustained in a flying accident, Dewar continued to fly regularly with his pilots.

When the Germans launched their offensive, on 10 May 1940, 87, based in the north of France, was soon in action under the leadership of Dewar and made more than 60 claims in the following weeks before being withdrawn to England on 22 May. Dewar opened his score on 11 May when he claimed the destruction of a Ju87 (and another the next day). For his leadership of his unit he received the double award of DSO and DFC on 31 May and became one of the first four officers to receive this double award. Continuing to lead 87 in the first stages of the Battle of Britain, he added more claims on 11 July. The next day he was promoted to Wing Commander and made Station Commander at Exeter. Despite his position, he continued to fly operationally from time to time with No. 213 Squadron and made more claims in August with the last, on the 25th, bringing his total to six confirmed victories (one shared) and two probables with maybe three more confirmed claims made in France. However, he was posted missing on 12 September flying a Hurricane (V7306) on a routine flight between Tangmere and Exeter.

A mixed fleet of two and three blade Hurricanes of No. 87 Sqn during the Phoney War in France. The squadron was based at Lille-Seclin in the North of France.

ESAU,
Ernest Arthur Roy,
RAAF

AUS. 405473

Australian

DFC

Ernest Esau, from Queensland, Australia, enlisted in March 1941. Trained in Australia and Canada, he sailed to the UK where he completed his training at No. 57 OTU. He was first posted to No. 129 Squadron then, in November, to **No. 453 (RAAF) Squadron** and became a Flight commander in May. On 2 December he shared in the destruction of a Ju88. This was his only claim. In May 1944, he was posted out as tour-expired. He received the DFC in August. He returned to the squadron in September for another tour as OC flying Spitfire Mk.IXs and then Mk.XVIs in the fighter-bomber role. He remained at the head of 453 until the end of war before relinqui-shing command in July. Repatriated in September, he was released from the RAAF in January 1946.

Extracted from a propaganda film, S/L Esau taxiing with his Spitfire Mk.XVI SM278/FU-?. It was common in this squadron to reserve the '?' for the CO. No. 453 was credited with 79.5 victories, confirmed and probable including 44 while flying the Brewster Buffalo in the Far East against the Japanese in 1941-42.

'Tony' Eyre enlisted in the AuxAF in 1938 and joined **No. 615 (County of Surrey) Squadron**. He was called to full-time service at the end of August 1939, with war looming, and was sent to France a couple of weeks later with the BEF. He made his first claims, on 19 May, two days before the squadron was withdrawn to the UK.

He continued to gain successes over German aircraft in the following weeks and when he was awarded the DFC at the end of August his tally had risen to 10 confirmed victories (two shared), two probables and six damaged. He became a Flight commander during the autumn and took command of the squadron in February 1941. He left in April at the end of his tour without having made further claims.

He returned to operations, in March 1942, as Wing Leader at **North Weald Wing**. On his first sortie, on the 8th, he was shot down by an Fw190 and was captured. He was eventually released in May 1945 after more than three years in captivity. He continued to serve in the RAF after the war but was killed flying a Tempest on 16 February 1946.

The wreckage of Tony Eyre's Spitfire Mk.V W3276/A-E after it had flipped over. Fortunately it happened at low speed and the tail prevented Eyre from being crushed underneath.

FINUCANE,
Brendan Eamonn Fergus, RAF

RAF No. 41276

Irish

DSO, DFC & Two Bars

'Paddy' Finucane was a Dubliner who joined the RAF in 1938. He completed his training just in time to participate in the Battle of Britain while flying with No. 65 Squadron. He made his first claims on 12 August, and more the next day, but made no more before the end of the Battle of Britain. His luck returned in January 1941 when he shot down more German aircraft and was posted to the newly formed No. 452 Squadron RAAF in April 1941 as a Flight commander. He was awarded the DFC the following month. While with 452, his tally rose steadily for the rest of the year to about 20 confirmed 'kills'. A Bar and a second Bar to his DFC followed within two weeks in September 1941 and, a rare award for a Flight Lieutenant fighter pilot, a DSO was received in October. The following month he was taken to the hospital for a broken ankle and didn't rejoin 452 until January 1942. It was only for a short time, however, as he was appointed CO of **No. 602 (City of Glasgow) Squadron** where he continued to add more victories to his tally (the last being on 8 June, a probable Fw190). Three weeks later he left 602 to become Wing Leader of the **Hornchurch Wing**. On 15 July 1942, while leading his Wing, his Spitfire's radiator (BM308) was hit by ground fire over France,. His engine eventually overheated and seized over the Channel. He tried to ditch his aircraft but it was seen to sink instantly upon hitting the sea. Finucane was never seen again. He was 21. He was credited with 32 confirmed victories (six shared), nine probably destroyed (one shared) and eight aircraft damaged.

Spitfire Mk.IIs of No. 452 (RAAF) Sqn at the time when Finucane was a Flight commander and had begun to build his name as an outstanding fighter pilot. In the spring of 1942, No. 452 was sent to Australia to defend Darwin against the Japanese raids. In all, the squadron was credited with 91 confirmed and probable destroyed aircraft against both the Germans and the Japanese.

FROST,
John Everitt, SAAF

SAAF No. P102641

South African

DSO, DFC & Bar

'Jack' Frost joined the South African Permanent Force in 1936. Serving at first as a flying instructor, he joined No. 1 Squadron SAAF early in 1939. When No. 3 Squadron SAAF was formed in September 1940, he was posted in as a Flight commander. This unit was sent to Eastern Africa to fight the Italians in 1941 and Frost made his first claim on 3 February by shooting down a Fiat CR.42 and three Ca.133s. This action earned him an immediate DFC. He served with this squadron until he was evacuated to hospital in May. At that time he had made about 10 claims against the Italians plus about 30 more on the ground.

In July he had recovered and was appointed OC **No. 5 Squadron SAAF** in the Western Desert in October and made further claims between March and June 1942 (mostly over the Gazala line and Bir Hakeim). However, on 16 June, he failed to return, in Tomahawk AN422, from an escort for Bostons, after a fight against the Bf109s of JG27. A Bar to his DFC was subsequently gazetted in August. Frost was the SAAF's top-scorer of WW2 with 16 confirmed victories (two shared), three probable (two shared) and three damaged (one shared).

Despite its shortcomings and being outclassed by 1942, the Tomahawk still equipped about half a dozen fighter squadrons in 1941-1942 including three SAAF squadrons. One of these was No. 5 Sqn (codes 'GL'). This unit was credited with 69 victories during the war (over 63 in the Western Desert). *(Michael Schoeman)*

GLEED,

**Ian Richard,
RAF**

RAF **No. 37800**

British

DSO, DFC

Ian Gleed joined the RAF before the war, in 1936, and his first assignment was No. 46 Squadron on completion of his training. In October 1939 he went to the newly formed No. 266 Squadron as a Flight commander and waited to be equipped with Spitfires. Injured in a flying accident in February 1940, he returned to the squadron in April in time to participate in the first air combats over France. He was posted to **No. 87 Squadron** on 14 May, flying Hurricanes based in France and, four days later, claimed two Bf110s destroyed. In the next two days he added six more aircraft (two being shared). He remained with 87 for the duration of the Battle of Britain, adding more claims, and a DFC followed in September 1940. At the end of the year he took charge of the squadron and led the unit until November 1941 while adding more successes in the same period of time. In November 1941 he became Wing Leader of the **Ibsley Wing**, flying Spitfires this time, and claimed two confirmed victories, two shared probable victories and one damaged aircraft as a Wing Commander. A DSO followed in May 1942 and he relinquished command in July. After various positions at HQs in the UK, he went to the Middle East in January 1943 and, by the end of the month, he became the WingCo flying of **No. 244 Wing**. At the head of his Wing, he made his final claims in March and April 1943 (the last on 6 April), giving a total of 16 confirmed victories (three shared), seven probables (three shared) and four damaged. Sadly, 10 days after his last claim, he was shot down and killed in his Spitfire (AB502) by a German fighter over Tunisia while attacking a large formation of Axis transport aircraft.

Ian Gleed flying off the Tunisian coast. Gleed is flying his Spitfire Mk.V, AB502/IR-G, in which he was shot down and killed on 16 April 1943.

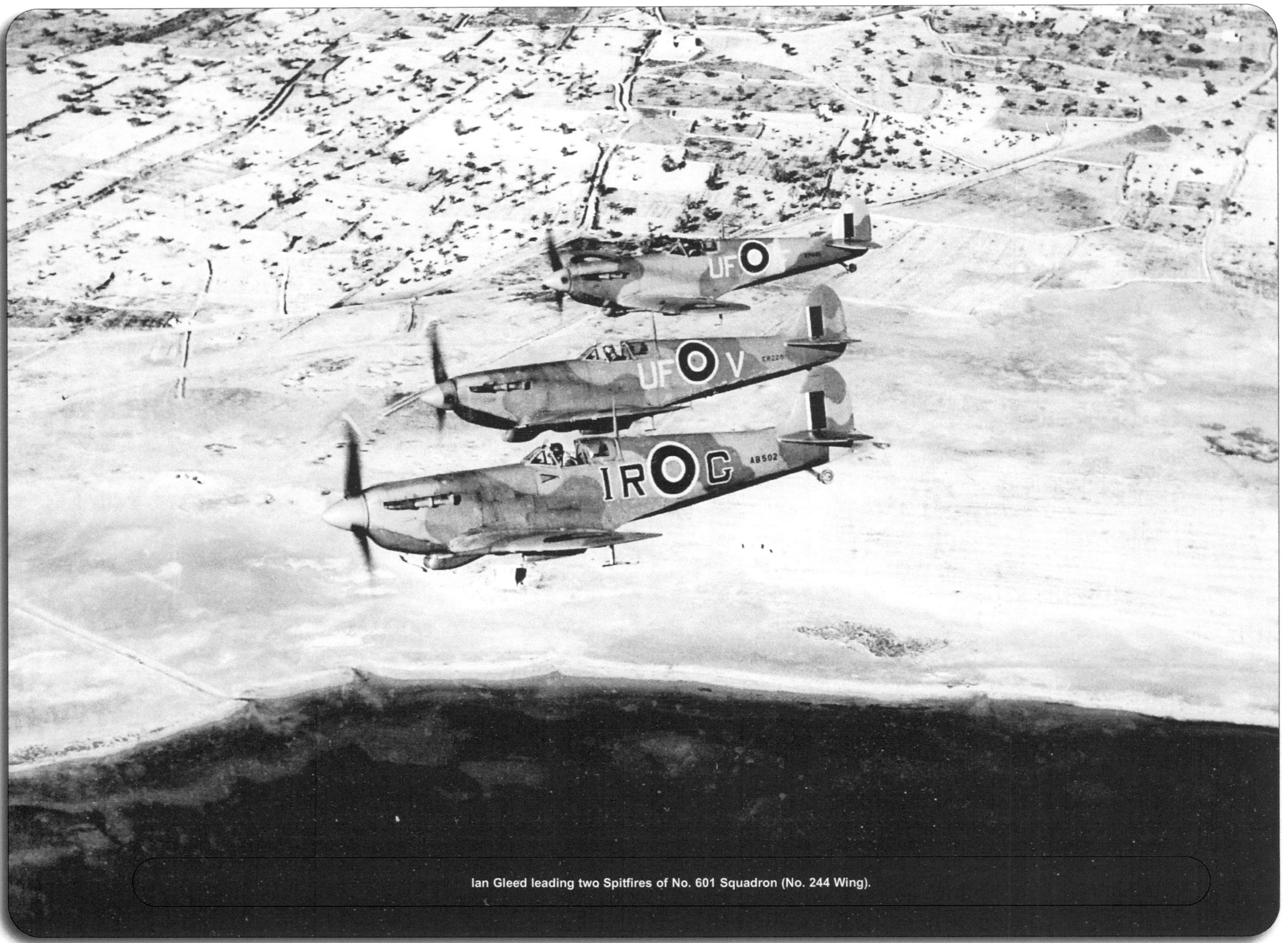

Ian Gleed leading two Spitfires of No. 601 Squadron (No. 244 Wing).

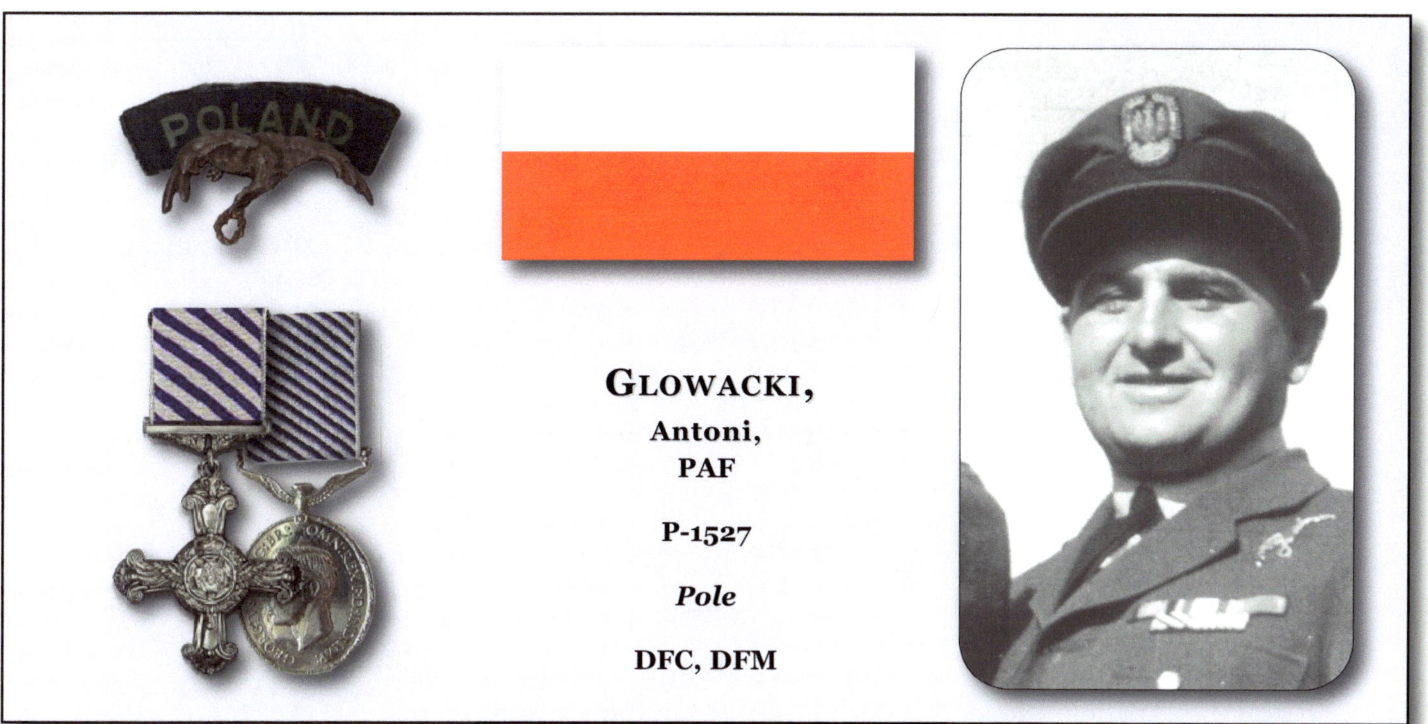

'Toni' Glowacki joined the Polish Air Force in 1930. He participated in the first combats against the Luftwaffe as a reconnaissance pilot in September 1939. He succeeded in escaping from Poland and arrived in England in January 1940. Re-trained as a fighter pilot, he was posted as an NCO to No. 501 (County of Gloucester) Squadron in August 1940 and was engaged in the Battle of Britain, making his first claim as early as 15 August. In February 1941, with eight confirmed 'kills' to his credit and a DFM awarded in October 1940, he left 501 to become an instructor before returning to operations, now commissioned, in October with No. 611 (West Lancashire) Squadron. Posted to No. 303 (Polish) Squadron the following month, he remained with 303 until February 1943, having added one shared victory and two German aircraft probably destroyed to his tally, when he was posted to No. 308 (Polish) Squadron as a Flight commander. A DFC followed in November that year. He was detached at various times to other units, including to the USAAF, until April 1944 when his second tour ended. When he returned to carry out a third tour in September, he was appointed to take command of **No. 309 (Polish) Squadron** shortly after its conversion to a fighter unit. He led 309 until the end of war. He remained with the RAF and, later, served with the RNZAF when he emigrated to New Zealand. He is credited with nine confirmed victories (one shared), three probables and five aircraft damaged.

When No. 309 Sqn, a former Army co-operation unit was converted to fighters, the unit was re-equipped with the Mustang Mk.III to carry out escort missions. By the end of the war, Toni Glowacki was flying KH574/WC-A. No. 309's pilots only claimed four confirmed before the end of the war but three of them were Me262 jet fighters!

GRACIE,
Edward John,
RAF

RAF No. 29090

British

DFC

'Jumbo' Gracie had been serving with the RAF since March 1937 when war broke out. In early 1940 he was posted to an operational unit, No. 79 Squadron. In June he was posted to No. 56 Squadron as a Flight commander where he made his first claim, a Bf110 destroyed, on 10 July. In July and August 1940 he added seven more confirmed victories (two being shared), two probables and two damaged aircraft but, on 30 August, he was shot down and injured. These injuries kept him away from the squadron for a couple of weeks. He returned in October and was awarded with the DFC. His tour eventually ended in January 1941 but no more claims were made before this date.

His rest was short as in March he was given command of **No. 23 Squadron** and, with his Blenheim Mk.IF, he claimed one probable Do17 on the night of 14/15 March. At the end of April he was posted back to a day fighter unit, **No. 601 (County of London) Squadron** as the OC. Later that year 601 was converted to the Airacobra Mk.I. He was to be the only officer to have led an Airacobra fighter squadron in the RAF. He finally left in December 1941 and, by the following spring, was fighting over Malta at the head of **No. 126 Squadron,** adding more claims, first on Hurricanes and later on Spitfires. At the end of April he became the Wing Commander of **Takali Wing** for the next two months, shortly after having made his final claim over a Ju87 destroyed on 23 April, which was shared. He returned to Britain in June 1942 with a score made now of 10 victories (three shared), five probables and six aircraft damaged. He briefly commanded **No. 32 Squadron** in September but his tour ended soon after. Another tour started in October 1943 when he joined **No. 169 Squadron**, flying Mosquito intruders, as the OC. He flew the unit's first sortie, since conversion to the Mosquito, on 20 January 1944, but he failed to return from an intruder op on 15/16 February while flying Mosquito NF.II HJ707, shot down by a night fighter.

No. 601 Squadron was unique during the war in that it was the only RAF fighter unit to fly the Airacobra in operations. Faced with a number of problems, the type was withdrawn from use and many were later given to the Soviets.

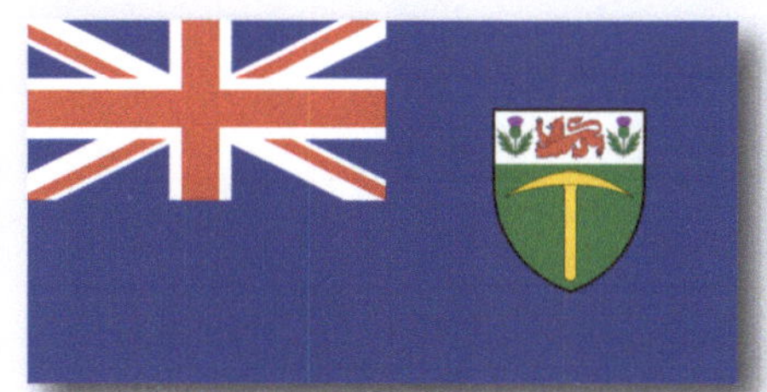

GREEN,
Charles Llewellyn,
RAF

RAF No. 41527

Rhodesian

DSO & Bar, DFC

From Southern Rhodesia, Charles Green enlisted in the RAF on a Short Service Commission in December 1938. At the beginning of the war, he was flying Ansons with No. 500 Squadron in Coastal Command. In early 1941 he was posted to No. 235 Squadron to fly Blenheim fighters. In June 1941 he was posted, along with many of the Rhodesian pilots in the RAF, to **No. 266 (Rhodesia) Squadron**. By September he had become one of the Flight commanders and, the following month, he opened his score by damaging a Bf109 before becoming the OC. He remained at the head of the squadron until July 1943 and oversaw the unit's transition to the Typhoon in March 1942. With this new fighter he added two confirmed victories (one shared) and one damaged. The latter, on 17 April, was his last claim and brought his total to three confirmed victories (two shared) and two aircraft damaged. He was also awarded the DFC in February 1943. He returned to operations, after a rest, in January 1944 as WingCo flying of **No. 121 Wing**. He kept this position until August 1944 when he became OC of **No. 124 Wing**. The following month, he was awarded the DSO and a Bar to that a month later. However, despite his rank of Group Captain, and therefore not allowed to fly on operations, on 26 December, 1944, while conducting a ground attack west of St-Vith, during the Battle of Bulge, his Typhoon was hit by flak and he baled out over enemy held territory and spent the rest of war as a PoW.

No. 266 Squadron was among the first squadrons to convert to Hawker Typhoon in January 1942. The 266 was one the three RAF squadrons to have been named 'Rhodesia' during the war with Nos. 44 and 237 Squadrons in which the majority Southern Rhodesian airmen served with during the war. A fourth squadron, also flying Typhoon was named 'Northern Rhodesia'. *(via Chris Thomas)*

Hawker Typhoon Mk IB MN666, W/C C.L. Green,
No. 121 Wing, Holmsley South, June 44

GUILLAUME,
Désiré Albert, RAF

RAF No. 102953

Belgian

DFC

'Guilly' Guillaume, born in 1901, was rather old for a fighter pilot when the war broke out. He had joined the Belgian army in 1918, transferred to the Air Component in 1921 and became a fighter pilot two years later. In 1940 he was a Major, in a non-flying posting, leading the Air Firing School but, soon after the French armistice, he decided to flee to the UK. After brief training he joined No. 131 (County of Kent) Squadron, where a Belgian flight had been formed, at the end of August 1941 but left it soon after in October to serve with No. 79 Squadron and then No.615 (County of Surrey) Squadron. In January 1942 he was posted to the newly formed **No. 350 (Belgian) Squadron** as B Flight commander. Two months later he became the first Belgian OC of the squadron. He relinquished his command in December to take charge of RAF Hornchurch. He had received a DFC the previous October. He ended the war as a Group Captain and Inspector of the Belgian Air Force in Great Britain.

Spitfire Mk.Vs of No. 350 Sqn in summer 1942 at the time S/L Guillaume was in command. No. 350 was credited with 57 confirmed and probable victories during the war.
(André Bar)

HAMPSHIRE,
Keith MacDermott, RAAF

AUS. 147

Australian

DSO & Bar, DFC

From New South Wales, Australia, Keith Hampshire was serving in the Far East as an officer in the RAAF when war broke out in September 1939. In September 1941, prior to the Japanese attack, he was given command of No. 6 Squadron RAAF, flying Hudsons based in New Guinea. In March 1942 he took control of No. 23 Squadron RAAF, still flying Hudsons, and, in December, he was appointed OC of No. 22 Squadron RAAF, flying Bostons. The squadron was the only RAAF unit to be equipped with this aircraft. He relinquished his command in July and was awarded the DSO. He was then posted to the UK during the summer of 1943, and, after a night fighter conversion course undertaken at No. 60 OTU from September, he was posted to the Mosquito-equipped **No. 456 (RAAF) Squadron** the following December. With his radar operator, T. Condon, they soon became a successful crew in claiming seven aircraft destroyed and one more probable between March and June 1944. In May he was awarded the DFC. He left the unit in November 1944, was promoted to Group Captain and posted to Transport Command in various positions before being repatriated in February 1946 and discharged in April. A Bar to his DSO was awarded in February 1945.

Coded 'RX', a Mosquito of No. 456 Sqn begins its patrol. The squadron used three main marks - the NF.II, NF.XVII and NF.30. This unit claimed 44 aircraft destroyed or probably destroyed (all but three in the Mosquito) in four years of existence.

HAWKINS,
Leonard Charles Cookson, RAF

RAF No. 102129

British

DFC

'Lee' Hawkins enlisted in the RAF in early autumn 1940. One year later he was posted to **No. 135 Squadron** which had been just reformed in August on Hurricanes. The squadron became operational in October but embarked for India the next month and was then re-routed to Burma, upon its arrival in January 1942, where it began operations at the end of the month against the Japanese. Hawkins saw action everywhere 135 was engaged and made his first claim on 5 March 1943. Others following during the month bringing his total to two confirmed victories, two probables and one aircraft damaged. At the end of the summer he had become a flight commander then, in March 1944, the OC. In May the squadron converted to the Thunderbolt and used the big fighter until the end of war. In November he was awarded the DFC and assumed command until the squadron being renumbered **No. 615 (County of Surrey) Squadron** on the 10 June 1945. But that would be for a short time only, being posted out before the end of the month.

Group Captain G.F. Chater (OC 902 Wing) conferring with Squadron Leader Lee Hawkins, kneeling, and other pilots of the squadron. The Thunderbolts have been newly-coded 'WK'. In the background, HB975/WK-L, usually flown by Hawkins, has five sortie markings ahead of the cockpit. As the aircraft completed its fifth mission on 25 October, and its sixth on the 28th, it is likely that this photo was taken between those two dates. No. 135 made all of its claims against the Japanese with all but one being made while flying the Hurricane.

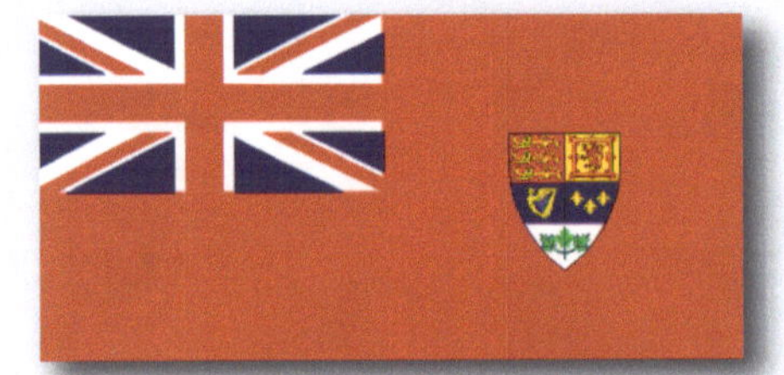

HILL,
George Urquart, RCAF

CAN./C. 1075

Canadian

DFC & Two Bars

George Hill, from Nova Scotia, joined the RCAF a few days after Canada had entered the war. Once his training was completed, he spent a couple of months in Canada as a flying instructor before sailing for the UK in January 1942. He was posted to No. 421 (RCAF) Squadron in April and, two months later, to the reforming No. 453 (RAAF) Squadron where a Flight Commander was needed. In August he moved to No. 403 (RCAF) Squadron where he made his first claims on 19 August over Dieppe during Operation 'Jubilee'. In December he was sent overseas and in February he joined **No. 111 Squadron**, participated to the Tunisian campaign, and was leading the squadron by the end of April. With this unit he made most of his claims, 16 confirmed, which led to a DFC in May 1943 and a Bar two weeks later. He left 111 in August 1943 and a second Bar was added to his DFC the following month. After some rest Hill returned to the front line as OC of the recently formed **No. 441 (RCAF) Squadron** in England in March 1944. On 25 April he claimed a shared victory over an Fw190. This was his last claim as his aircraft was damaged during the same combat and he was forced to make an emergency landing in France. He first evaded capture but was eventually captured and spent the rest of the war in a PoW camp. He was released in May 1945 and left the RCAF the following September. He is credited with 18 confirmed victories (eight shared), three probables and ten aircraft damaged.

For his second tour, Hill was given the command of the new Canadian No. 441 Sqn (codes '9G') in March. It was only for a short time, however, as he was shot down the following month. No. 441 was credited with 48 confirmed victories in over a year of existence.

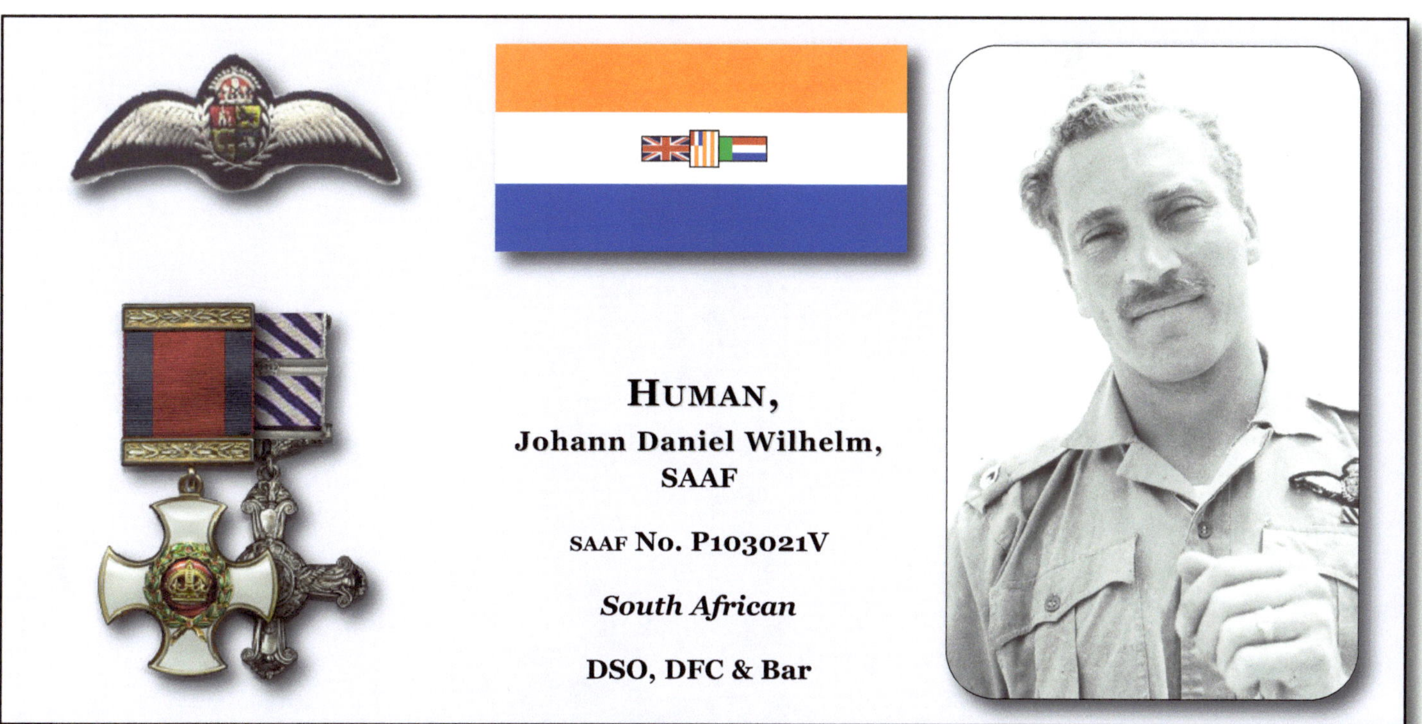

HUMAN,
Johann Daniel Wilhelm, SAAF

SAAF No. P103021V

South African

DSO, DFC & Bar

Joining the SAAF as a regular officer in 1939, 'Johnny' Human received his wings in December of that year. He first served in East Africa with No. 40 Squadron SAAF, a tactical reconnaissance unit, in 1940-1941, completed 77 sorties and received a DFC in March 1941 for his actions. Later in the year he was posted to the Western Desert as a fighter pilot, flying Tomahawks with No. 5 Squadron SAAF. On 11 March 1942 he succeeded in damaging a Ju88, his first claim, although he shared his success with another pilot. Nonetheless, a couple of days later, he received orders to join **No. 2 Squadron SAAF** as a Flight commander and eventually became its OC at the end of May. He shot down two Bf109s around the same time. At the end of July he left the squadron with a Bar to his DFC. After a period of rest he returned to operations in April 1943 with No. 5 Squadron SAAF as supernumerary Major. Here he made his final claim, a Me323 on 22 April, bringing his total to five confirmed victories and one shared aircraft damaged. His stay with No. 5 Squadron was short as at the beginning of May he was posted to **No. 7 Wing SAAF** and stayed there until October. He temporarily led the Wing between May and July 1943. In May 1944 he returned once more to operations, officially this time as OC of the Wing, and held this position until April 1945 having been awarded the DSO in March and promoted to full Colonel in January. He returned to South Africa to take charge of No. 11 OTU SAAF.

When No. 2 Squadron SAAF converted to Kittyhawk in May 1942, its squadron codes were changed from TA to DB. Here an early Kittyhawk Mk. I, AK840 in May 1942. This squadron would continue to use the Mk I until June 1942.
(Michael Schoeman)

Supermarine Spitfire Mk IX MH944, Col J.D.W. Human,
No. 7 Wing SAAF, Forli, Italy, January 1945

HUNTER,
Philip Algernon, RAF

RAF No. 32081

British

DSO

Philip Hunter joined the RAF in 1931 on a short service commission. In 1939 he was serving on the staff of the Central Flying School and was appointed OC of **No. 264 Squadron** in March 1940 just a few days after the squadron had been declared operational on the new Boulton Paul Defiant.

The Defiant went into action over the continent in May 1940 during the first days of the German invasion. Hunter and his gunner, LAC Frederic H. King, were the first to make a claim on the Defiant on 12 May. More victories were added to their tally before the end of the month with 10 confirmed (one shared) and one probable. Leading the squadron for the month, in which 264 claimed more than 65 confirmed victories, his actions were rewarded with a DSO in June 1940. It is worth noting that Hunter played a major role in improving the combat tactics of the Defiant during the first engagements. Hunter continued to lead 264 during the Battle of Britain but by now the Germans had discovered the weakness of the Defiant and the aircraft sustained heavy losses including Hunter, who was lost in action on 24 August 1940, in Defiant N1535. The Defiant was withdrawn from day fighter operations one month later.

Squadron Leader Hunter, in Defiant N1535/PS-A, leading a patrol during July 1940. At that time the RAF was still confident in the capabilities of the Defiant as day fighter. Two months later its career as a day fighter was over. No. 264 was credited with about 150 victories during the war with close to 105 on the Defiant and 90 of those at day.

JOHNSON,
James Edgar, RAF

RAF No. 83267

British

DSO & Two Bars, DFC & Bar

'Johnnie' Johnson was the Commonwealth's top-scorer of WW2. After various attempts, Johnson was finally accepted into the RAF in August 1939. Completing his training, he was first posted to No. 19 Squadron in August 1940 before moving to No. 616 (South Yorkshire) Squadron the following month. He made his first claim on 15 January 1941 sharing a Do17 as damaged. By the end of September his tally had increased steadily which included a double claim on 21 September, and he was awarded the DFC that same month. By that time he was acting as a flight commander. In June 1942 a Bar to his DFC was added. The next month he left the squadron to take command of **No. 610 (County of Chester) Squadron**. He remained in this position until March 1943 when he left to lead the **Kenley Wing**. On 15 June, he made a second double claim over Fw019s and the same month he was awarded the DSO and a Bar followed in September before he was sent for a rest for the next six months.

In March 1944 he returned to operations and, posted as Wing Leader, led **No. 144 (RCAF) Wing** during the Normandy landings. He had claimed another ten victories by July including three double claims (5 April, 28 June and 5 July). When the wing was disbanded in mid-july, he became the WingCo Flying of **No. 127 (RCAF) Wing** and earned a second Bar to his DSO in the meantime and adde another double claim on 23 August. He made his last claim with this unit on 27 September, a Bf109 destroyed to bring his total to 41 confirmed victories (seven shared), five probables (two shared) and 13 damaged (three shared). He led the Wing until March 1945 when he was promoted to Group Captain and was appointed as OC of **No. 125 Wing** until the end of the war.

He remained with the RAF after the war and retired as an Air Vice-Marshal in March 1966.

On moving to No. 125 Wing, Johnson adopted this Spitfire Mk.XIV, MV258/JEJ as his personal aircraft.
(Andrew Thomas)

Wing Command 'Johnny' Johnson at Bazenville Landing Ground in Normandy on 31 July 1944. At that taime his score was 35.

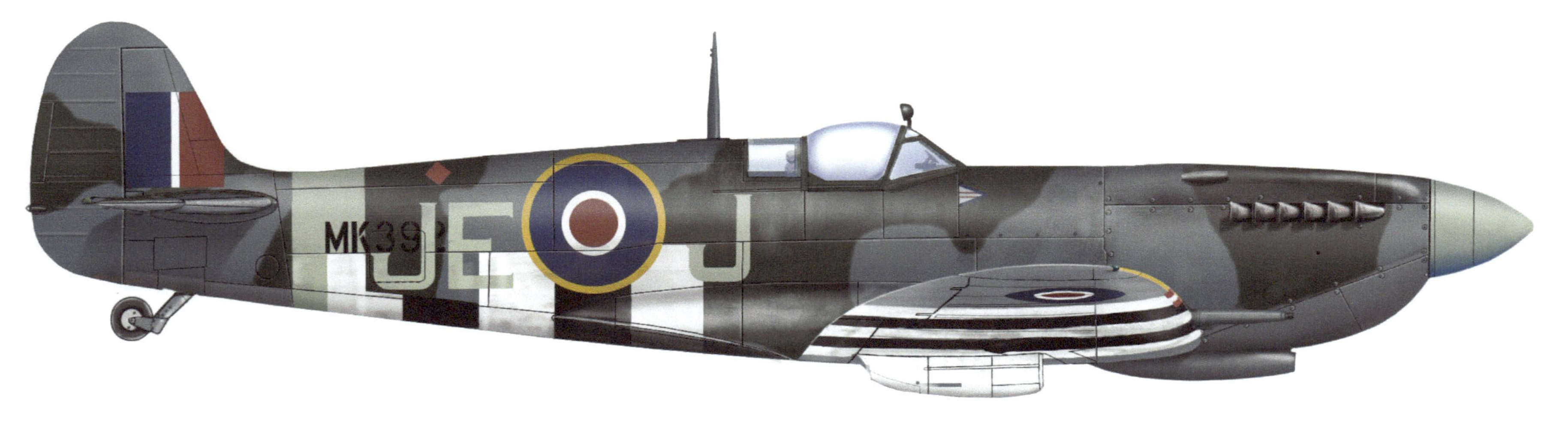

Supermarine Spitfire Mk IX MK392, W/C J.E. Johnson,
No. 127 Wing, B.2 Bazenville, France, July 1944

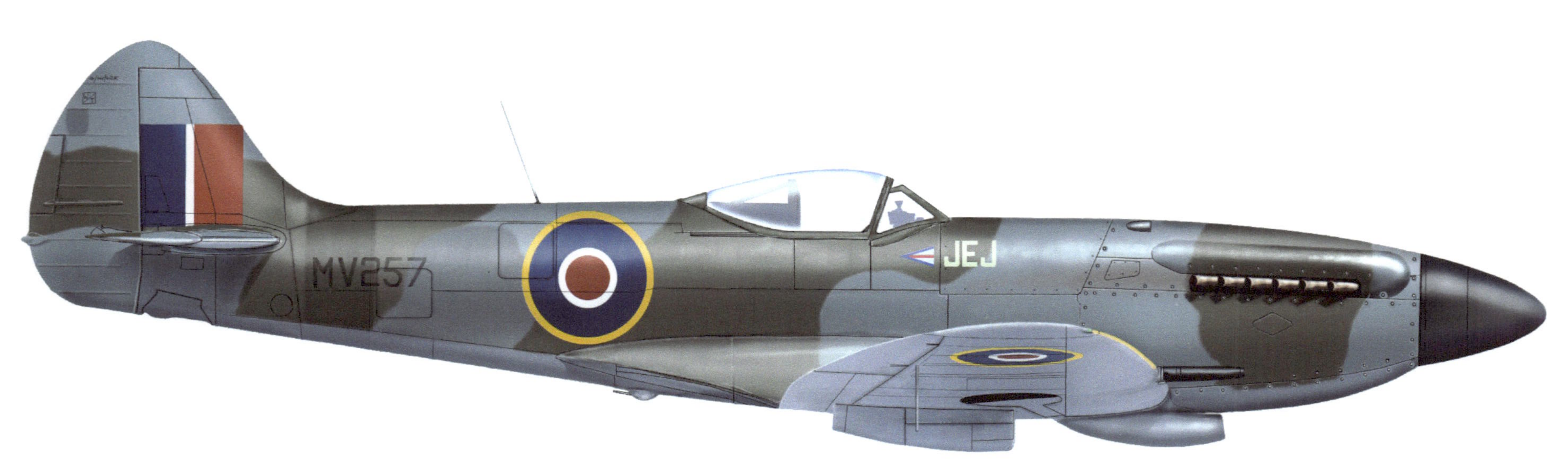

Supermarine Spitfire Mk XIV MV257, G/C J.E. Johnson,
No. 125 Wing, Kastrup, Denmark, May 1945

KALLIO,
**Oliver Charles,
RCAF**

CAN./ J.6494

American

DSO, DFC

'Sandy' Kallio was an American from Michigan. Before the war he served with the USAAC and in June 1940 he crossed the Canadian border to enlist in the RCAF. At almost 30 Kallio was already considered as old for a fighter pilot. Initially trained in Canada, he completed his training in England and was sent overseas to join, in March 1942, No. 33 Squadron which was flying Hurricanes in the Western Desert. On 2 June he opened his score by damaging a Bf109. When he became a flight commander in September, he had added another damaged aircraft to his credit but scored three more times before the end of the year. He received the DFC in January 1943. In May, tour expired, he was sent for a rest. In September he started another tour with No. 601 (County of London) Squadron and remained there for two months before being called to lead **No. 145 Squadron** where he would go on to make more claims. However, on 20 February, he broke a leg when his aircraft crashed on return from a patrol and was obliged to give up his command. Two days previously, he had shot down an Fw190, his last claim, to bring his total to four aircraft destroyed, one probable and four damaged. Recovering from his injury, he was appointed OC of **No. 417 (RCAF) Squadron** in June and held this position until November. It was his last operational posting. He was awarded the DSO the following January.

Spitfire Mk.VIII (JF503), of No. 145 Sqn, under maintenance in Italy in February 1944 at the time when Kallio was forced to give up command after his accident.

KNIGHT,
Marcus William Bower, RAF

RAF No. 37408

New Zealander

DFC

Marcus Knight left New Zealand in 1935 to join the RAF. After his training he became a flying instructor and was still an instructor, a Flight commander of No. 5 Service Flight Training School with more than 1,000 hours of flying experience, when the war broke out. After the Battle of Britain the RAF was short of fighter pilots so, to help replace those who had been killed, injured or posted away for rest, he was sent, in December 1940, to undertake fighter training at No. 57 OTU. In January 1941 he was posted to No. 257 (Burma) Squadron as a flight commander. The next month he was transferred to No. 310 (Czech) Squadron, again as a Flight commander, and in March he was given the task of forming the first New Zealand fighter unit in the RAF, **No. 485 (NZ) Squadron**. He was a good candidate and in a month, had the squadron operational. Then on 2 June, 1941, he shot down the first German aircraft claimed by the New Zealanders. In October he added a damaged claim to his credit and was awarded the DFC. At the end of November 1941 he relinquished command of the squadron. No more operational postings followed and he served in various administrative positions in the UK and Middle East. He was a Group Captain at the cessation of hostilities. He remained in the RAF after the war.

In the background, Squadron Leader Knight's Spitfire Mk.VB, coded OU-Z (AB870), of No. 485 Sqn seen here at Redhill during the summer of 1941. Some of the squadron's early Spitfire Mk.Vs were funded by New Zealand and it's Pacific Island protectorates.
(via P. Sorthehaug - both)

KUHLMANN,
Keith Cowie,
SAAF

SAAF No. P102441V

South African

DFC

Joining the SAAF in July 1940, as a regular officer, Kuhlmann was posted to the UK early in 1942 on conclusion of his training in Southern Rhodesia. He was part of the first batch of fighter pilots who had volunteered for service with the RAF in the United Kingdom at the end of 1941. He served with No. 222 (Natal) Squadron but, in August 1942, he sailed for Malta where he was posted to No. 185 Squadron. A few days after his arrival he opened his score by shooting down a Ju88 on the 27th. Other claims followed over the coming weeks (he added three more aircraft destroyed, one probable and three damaged) until 19 October, the date of his last claim. When he left Malta, at the end of January 1943, he had become a Flight commander and a DFC was gazetted the following March.

After a period of rest at No. 57 OTU, he was posted at the end of August to **No. 322 (Dutch) Squadron** as Officer Commanding. Without making any further claims, he led the unit until 1 September 1944 when his Spitfire Mk. IX was shot down by flak during an armed reconnaissance. He was taken prisoner and was released at the end of the war. He continued to serve in the SAAF after the war and retired as a Brigadier in 1973.

During the summer of 1944, No. 322 Sqn was re-equipped with the Griffon-engined Spitfire Mk.XIV with which they hunted the V-1s. Kuhlmann used to fly this one, NH718/3W-G. No. 332 made no confirmed or probable claims during the war but shot down about 120 V-1s.
(Michael Schoeman)

LANE,
Brian John Edward, RAF

RAF No. 37859

British

DFC

'Sandy' Lane joined the RAF on a short service commission in 1936. When war broke out he was serving with No. 213 Squadron but was posted to **No. 19 Squadron** soon after as a flight commander.

He was engaged over the sky of Dunkirk in May 1940 and claimed his first success on 26 May shortly after having taken temporary command of the squadron due to the death of the CO on the 25th. He made more claims in the following days and, for his actions over Dunkirk, he received a DFC in July. In September he was appointed OC of the squadron for a second time, this time permanently, having gained enough experience to lead in his own right. He remained at the head of 19 until June 1941. By then he was credited with seven confirmed victories (one shared), two unconfirmed victories, one probable and one aircraft damaged.

He was posted to the Middle East and served in various HQ positions before returning to Britain in June 1942 to take command of No. 61 OTU. He returned then to operations joining No. 167 Squadron, formed with one Dutch flight as supernumerary Squadron Leader. Sadly, four days after his arrival, on 13 December, he was shot down in his Spitfire (AR612/3W-U) during a dogfight with Fw190s over the Dutch coast.

Spitfire Mk.I P9368 of No. 19 Sqn during the Battle of Britain. This aircraft was often flown by Lane who claimed four of his victories when flying this aircraft. No. 19 was credited with about 170 confirmed and probable victories (70% of them on Spitfires). The squadron was later converted on to Mustangs in 1944.

LE MESURIER,
Gerald John,
SAAF

SAAF No. P102636V

South African

DFC

'Lemmie' Le Mesurier joined the SAAF in September 1936 to become a regular officer of the Permanent Force. At the outbreak of war, he was a flying instructor and in November he was posted as a flight commander to **No. 1 Squadron SAAF** fighting the Italians in East Africa. Flying Gladiators, he made his first claims in January and February 1941 with two Fiat CR.42s destroyed and another damaged. He left the squadron by mid-1941 having twice led it temporarily.

After a period of rest he returned to the squadron one year later. The unit was now in the Western Desert flying Hurricanes. He soon added one Ju87 destroyed on 3 July to his credit, and a probable the next day, but was wounded in action. His wounds kept him away from the squadron for a couple of weeks. He returned to operations in October and took command of the squadron. However, because he had not fully recovered from his wounds, he was sent back to the Union in November as medically unfit for further operational flying. He was awarded the DFC in April 1943. He travelled to Britain soon afterwards but was killed in a flying accident, on 8 July 1943, while practicing dive-bombing in a Master. His aircraft (W8453) collided with an Oxford.

In September 1942 No. 1 Sqn SAAF began to receive the cannon-armed Hurricane Mk.IIc. The same year, the codes 'AX' had been allocated to the squadron. This squadron remains the top SAAF fighter squadron scorer with more than 190 confirmed and probable victories during WW2. *(Michael Schoeman)*

LE ROY DU VIVIER,
Daniel Albert Raymond Georges,
RAF

RAF No. 82159

Belgian

DFC & Bar

Daniel Le Roy du Vivier was an NCO pilot with the Belgian *Aéronautique Militaire* when the Germans launched their offensive on Belgium and the Low Countries on 10 May 1940. He moved to France with his unit a couple of days later and on 19 June he left for the United Kingdom. Arriving in early July, he joined **No. 43 Squadron** in August 1940, after a short refresher course at No. 7 OTU, and claimed his first victory on 16 August against a Ju87 (plus another damaged). Wounded in combat on 2 September, he recovered to be posted to No. 229 Squadron where he made further claims (two probables, one shared) before returning to No. 43 Squadron to become a flight commander in April. More successes were recorded the following month. On 15 January 1942 he was finally appointed OC of the squadron thus becoming the first non-British Commonwealth pilot to command an RAF unit. He had been awarded the DFC a couple of days previously. On 28 May he claimed a Ju88 destroyed, his last claim, to bring his total to five confirmed victories (two shared), two probably destroyed (one shared) and one damaged. In September 1942 he relinquished command and a Bar to his DFC was added two months later. After various non-operational postings he was sent to the Middle East in April 1943 and posted to an HQ position. In June he went to No. 239 Wing as supernumerary Wing Commander to gain experience as a Wing Leader, but had a ground accident on 31 July that kept him away from flying for several months. In January 1944, he was authorised to return to operations and after a couple of weeks at No. 239 Wing, he became WingCo flying of **No. 324 Wing** in March 1944. This was his last operational posting before the end of the war. He returned to the UK in July 1944 and became the OC of No. 53 OTU the following month, a position he held until May 1945. He returned to civilian life in September 1946.

Hurricane Mk IIs of No. 43 squadron (code FT) at Tangmere in August 1942 at the time when Le Roy du Viver was the Officer Commanding.

Supermarine Spitfire Mk IX MJ628, W/C D.A.R.G. Le Roy du Vivier, No. 324 Wing, Nettuno (Anzio), Italy, May 1944

MACKIE,
Evan Dall,
RNZAF

NZ41520

New Zealander

DSO, DFC & Bar

'Rosie' Mackie joined the RNZAF in January 1941 and, upon completion of training in Canada, sailed to the UK in August 1941. He attended No. 58 OTU and was posted to No. 485 Squadron RNZAF in December 1941. He opened his score on 26 March 1942, by sharing in the destruction of a Bf109, and added one probable Fw190 the following month. He was posted to the Middle East in January 1943, joined **No. 243 Squadron** in March, and became a flight commander the next month. Within a couple of weeks Mackie achieved considerable success by claiming a 13 confirmed victories (one being shared) by September. He received a DFC in May and a Bar to this in September. He was promoted to lead the squadron in June. He left 243 in November to take command of

No. 92 (East India) Squadron, which he would lead until February 1944, and three more claims during this time. He returned to the UK for a rest and began a second tour of operations in December 1944 with No. 3, then No. 274 Squadron before taking charge of **No. 80 Squadron** in January 1945. Leading this unit until April 1945, he made his last claim on the 15th to bring his total to 23 confirmed victories (three shared), two probables and 10 damaged (one shared). Then he was called to become WingCo flying of **No. 122 Wing** where he ended the war. He was awarded the DSO in May 1945. He remained with the wing until September 1945 and then returned to New Zealand in October 1946.

Spitfires IX of No. 243 Squadron (code SN) at the time Mackie was leading the squadron during the summer 1943. The 243 received its first Spitfire Mk IX in June 1943.

Hawker Tempest Mk V SN228, W/C E.D. Mackie,
No. 122 Wing, B.152 Fassberg, Germany, summer 1945

Munro,
John Gray,
RAF

RAF No. 36016

British

-

John Munro joined the RAF with a direct-entry commission in September 1934. This was one of the few offered in competition each year to graduates of British and Commonwealth universities (Cambridge in Munro's case).

Upon completing his training, he was posted to No. 47 Squadron at Khartoum (Sudan). He returned to the UK in February 1936 and was posted to the Aircraft Armament Co-operation Flight. Later, in 1937, Munro went to the Air Armament School and moved to Research and Development in the Air Ministry in August 1938 where he was associated with the design of servo-fed 20mm cannons (later installed in RAF fighters). He maintained in this position until being sent to No. 5 OTU in June 1940 for a refresher course and conversion to Hurricanes. He was posted to

No. 263 Squadron as a Squadron Leader in mid-July 1940 but was immediately detached to the Air Ministry. Returning to the squadron three weeks later, his knowledge of 20mm cannons helped the Whirlwind, which was equipped with four such guns and new to the RAF, to become operational by the end of the year. In December 1940 he eventually took command of the squadron and led it until March 1941 when he went to the Aircraft Gun Mounting Establishment as Chief Test Pilot and Chief Technical Officer. Munro then spent the rest of war in various RAF technical positions and finally in a series of staff jobs in the UK and India from July 1943 onwards as a Wing Commander. Munro served in the RAF until 1949 and retired as a Group Captain.

Whirlwind P6969/HE-V when the type had just become operational with No. 263 Squadron. P6979/HE-Q was Munro's aircraft, his temporary presence on the squadron being due to his expertise with the 20mm Hispano-Suiza cannon armament. From January 1944 No. 263 converted to Typhoons. Its pilots made a dozen claims in all.

O'Meara, James Joseph, RAF

RAF No. 40844

British

DSO, DFC & Bar

James 'Orange' O'Meara joined the RAF on a short service commission in April 1938. At the outbreak of war he was serving with No. 64 Squadron and made his first claim, an unconfirmed Ju88, over Dunkirk. More successes followed including two Ju87s on 29 July and in September 1940 he was posted to No.72 Squadron and received a DFC at the same time in recognition of his six victories. He stayed with 72 for a short time before moving to 421 Flight (the future No. 91 Squadron) in October and added a Bar to his DFC in March 1941 for he had now doubled his claims. In October he was sent for a rest.

After having served briefly with No. 164 Squadron he started a new tour in January 1943 as a Squadron Leader and took command of **No. 131 (County of Kent) Squadron** in March and made his final claim on 3 August, a Fw190 damaged. He led 131 until May 1944 and for his actions was awarded the DSO in the following October. No more operational postings followed after May 1944. He survived the war with about 13 confirmed victories (two shared), one unconfirmed victory, four probables and 12 damaged (one shared).

When O'Meara left the 131, the squadron had recently converted to the rare Spitfire Mk VII. Number 131 Squadron was credited with 20 victories during the war.
(Paul Sorthaug)

Supermarine Spitfire Mk VII, S/L J.J. O'Meara,
No. 131 (County of Kent) Squadron, Culmhead, UK, May 1944

ORZECHOWSKI,
Jerzy,
RAF

RAF **No. 76825**

Pole

DFC

Jerzy Orzechowski enlisted in the pre-war Polish Air Force in 1925 and served as an observer. At the end of the thirties he was sent to study sciences at various places (including in France). When war broke out, as a captain, he was called to serve in a reconnaissance unit which was later withdrawn to Romania. From there he went to France and, at his own request, to Great Britain where he enlisted in the RAF.

He was retrained as a fighter pilot and, on completion of his training in September 1940, he was posted to No. 303 (Polish) Squadron. Further squadron moves followed in the next few weeks - No. 607 (County of Durham) Squadron, 306 (Polish) Squadron, No. 245 Squadron and 615 (County of Surrey) Squadron before he eventually arrived at **No. 308 (Polish) Squadron** as supernumerary Squadron Leader in December. Taking command of the squadron in February 1941, he led the unit until the end of his first tour in June.

Before starting another tour he chose to become a night fighter pilot and attended a course at No. 51 OTU. First posted to No. 23 Squadron, he was given command of **No. 307 (Polish) Squadron** in April 1943 (the only Polish night fighter squadron in the RAF). Flying Mosquito Mk.IIs, he made all of his claims in a single night when he probably destroyed a Bf110 and damaged three others. He relinquished command in November 1943 and was awarded the DFC in May 1944. Thereafter, only non-operational positions followed. He remained with the RAF until the disbandment of the PAF and emigrated to Canada later on.

Mosquito HJ932/EW-L during a patrol in 1943. No. 307 Sqn claimed 37.75 confirmed and probable victories with nearly half being claimed while flying the Mosquito Mk.II. *(Wilhelm Ratuszynski)*

 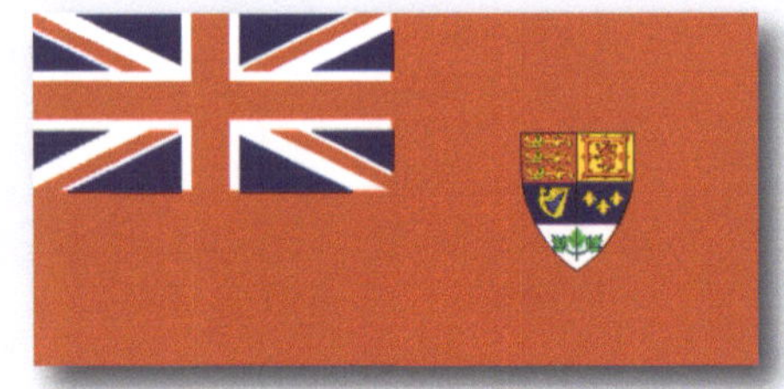

PLAMONDON,
Joseph Marie Guy,
RCAF

CAN./ J.8921

Canadian

DFC & Bar

Guy 'Plum' Plamondon (sometimes referred to as Joseph Plamondon), from the province of Quebec, enlisted in the RCAF in February 1941. Trained in Canada, he received his wings in November but was first retained in Canada and was not sent overseas until May 1943. In September he was posted to No. 198 Squadron where nearly half of the pilots were Canadians at the time. On 13 January 1944 he made his first claims when he shot down a Ju88 and shared in the destruction of an Ar96. In February 1944 he became a flight commander and participated in the first stage of the battle of Normandy with 198 before leaving it in July shortly after making his last claim, a Bf109 near Caen, to bring his total to three confirmed victories (one shared). He took command of

No. 193 Squadron at the end of the following month and in September he received a DFC for his service with No. 198 Squadron. He ended his tour in November and received a Bar to his DFC in February. He was repatriated in July 1945 and was released the following September.

'Plum' Plamondon ended his operational tour with No. 193 Sqn (formed in December 1942 and operational on Typhoons in April 1943). Despite its fighter-bomber role, its pilots managed to claim about eight confirmed or probable victories in two years.
(via Chris Thomas)

RATTEN,
John Richard,
RAAF

AUS. 405111

Australian

DFC

John Ratten was a Tasmanian who enlisted in the RAAF in January 1941. He completed his training in Canada and in the autumn of 1941 he sailed for the UK. After the completion of his course at No. 53 OTU, he was posted to No. 72 Squadron in February 1942. With this squadron he made his first claims - one damaged aircraft on 17 May and one confirmed victory on 31 May. In August, he was posted as flight commander to **No. 453 (RAAF) Squadron** and became its OC in November. In January 1943, after having attended the Fighter Leader's course, he left the squadron the following May to become the WingCo of the **Hornchurch Wing**. He thus became the first Australian Empire Air Training Scheme trainee to command a Spitfire wing in Great Britain. During his stay with 453 he could only add a damaged aircraft to his tally. As Wing Commander, however, he made more claims, increasing his score to four confirmed victories (two shared), three probables (one shared) and two aircraft damaged. The last of his claims was made on 4 July and at the end of this month he left the Wing as tour-expired. He had been awarded the DFC in June. He then became the Station Commander of Peterhead until May 1944. Once again, it was the first time that an Australian EATS graduate was to command an RAF Station. After May 1944 he was given command of No. 11 PDRC in charge of managing Australian personnel located in UK. He relinquished his command in January 1945 and was about to be repatriated when he died suddenly of pulmonary tuberculosis on 27 February.

A Spitfire Mk.V, of No. 453 Sqn and coded FU-Q (W3574), seen at dispersal at the end of 1942. After having fought against the Japanese on Buffaloes, where its pilots claimed about 40 aircraft destroyed or probably destroyed, the unit was re-formed in 1942 in Britain and made about 35 more claims flying Spitfires until the end of war.

RUSSEL,
Blair Dalzel,
RCAF

CAN./ C.1319

Canadian

DSO, DFC & Bar

From Toronto, Ontario, 'Dal' Russel, having learned to fly before the war, was directly commissioned into the RCAF in No. 115 Squadron (Auxiliary) RCAF on 15 September 1939. He completed his training in May 1940 and, when the squadron was disbanded, its personnel were absorbed by No. 1 Squadron RCAF which was to be sent to the UK. This squadron participated in the Battle of Britain and Russel made his first claim on 26 August. Other claims followed over the next month (over 10 of all kinds) and he received a DFC in October (one of the first three RCAF members to be awarded decorations during WW2). He returned to Canada in February 1941 and the following month became a Flight commander with No. 118 Squadron RCAF which had just reformed with Grumman Goblin fighters. In January 1942 he was appointed OC of **No. 14 Squadron RCAF**, flying the more modern Curtiss Kittyhawk, and relinquished command in December. He was then sent back to Britain, serving with various RCAF fighter units as a supernumerary Squadron Leader, before taking command of **No. 411 (RCAF) Squadron** in mid-April 1943. He left this unit in July to become the first WingCo flying of **No. 126 (RCAF) Wing**. In October he was posted to the RCAF Overseas HQ and received a Bar to his DFC the following month. In April 1944 he reverted to the rank of Squadron Leader to become OC of **No. 442 (RCAF) Squadron** and he led this unit until July. During this time he added one more claim. He was then called to lead again No. 126 (RCAF) Wing and did so until January 1945. While with the Wing he made his last claim, a Bf109 damaged on 10 August, to bring his total to seven confirmed victories (five shared), two probables and four damaged. Number 126 Wing was his last operational posting and he was awarded the DSO after the war for his service at the head of this unit. He returned to civilian life in July 1945.

'Dal' Russel served during the Battle of Britain with No. 1 Sqn RCAF which was renumbered No. 401 (RCAF) Squadron on 1 March 1941. As No. 1 Squadron it had made 36 confirmed or probable claims, all during the Battle of Britain.

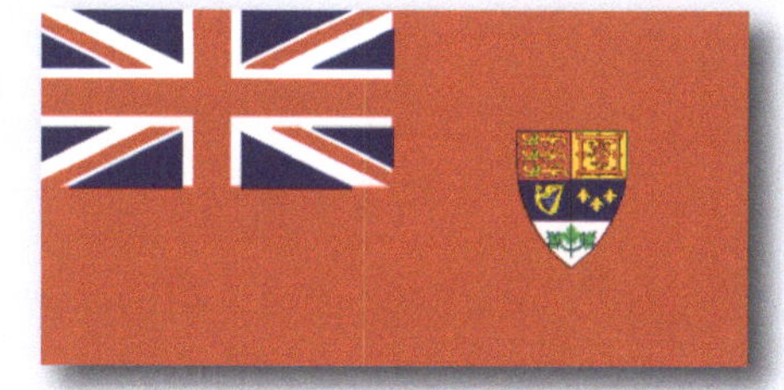

SAGER,
Arthur Hazelton,
RCAF

CAN./ **J.8683**

Canadian

DFC

'Art' Sager, from British Columbia, enlisted in the RCAF in February 1941. At the end of the year, with his commission and wings, he was shipped to the UK and, after completing his training at No. 58 OTU, he was posted to No. 421 (RCAF) Squadron in April 1942. On 11 June 1943 he opened his score by claiming a probable Bf109. It was followed by two damaged claims in July before he was posted to No. 416 (RCAF) Squadron in August. He remained with 416 until the end of his tour in January 1944 having added five confirmed (two shared) and one damaged aircraft to his score. He started another tour in August 1944, joining No. 403 (RCAF) Squadron, before returning to 416 in September where he made further claims (one confirmed victory and one shared damaged). At the end of the month he was appointed OC of **No. 443 (RCAF) Squadron** which had lost its CO - S/L McLeod - three days previously. A DFC followed in December. He led the unit until the end of March 1945 and returned to Canada two months later. He is credited with six confirmed victories (two shared), one probable and three damaged aircraft (one shared).

S/L 'Art' Sager leading the formation in TB476/2I-D 'Ladykiller'. When this photo was taken, Sager was in the last days of his command and was about to hand over to Thomas De Courcy. No. 443 Sqn was credited with 38 confirmed and probable victories.

SKALSKI,
Stanislaw,
RAF

RAF No. 76710

Pole

DSO, DFC & Two Bars

Stanislaw Skalski joined the pre-war Polish Air Force in 1936.When the war broke out he was a fighter pilot flying the PZL P.11c with the 142 Esk. In September 1939 he claimed no less than six German aircraft destroyed and one more as damaged. He withdrew with his unit to Romania and from there he chose to escape to England. He arrived in January 1940. He was re-trained and in August, in the middle of the Battle of Britain, he was posted to No. 302 (Polish) Squadron but, as the unit was not yet operational, he was re-routed to No. 501 (County of Gloucester) Squadron where he made about nine more claims in a couple of days. However, he was shot down and severely wounded on 5 September and was only able to return to the squadron six weeks later. In March 1941 he was posted to No. 306 (Polish) Squadron, flying Spitfires, and left in September as a Flight commander with five more confirmed victories and a DFC to his credit. He began a second tour in March 1942 with No. 316 (Polish) Squadron but left in May to take command of **No. 317 (Polish) Squadron** where he remained until the end of his tour in November. He left with a Bar to his DFC. Early in 1943, he took command of the special **Polish Fighting Team** of volunteers destined to go to North Africa with Spitfire Mk.IXs. Attached to No. 145 Squadron, this unit encountered considerable successes. When the unit was disbanded he was given command of **No. 601 (County of London) Squadron** in June 1943. He relinquished command in September and, the next month, he added a second Bar to his DFC. Returning to the UK, he was posted as WingCo flying to **No. 131 (Polish) Wing** in October and then **No. 133 (Polish) Wing**, equipped with Mustangs, in April 1944. Flying over the landings at Normandy, he made his last two claims on 24 June, two Bf109s destroyed, raising his total to twenty-four confirmed victories, one probable and five aircraft damaged. In August he was awarded the DSO and left the Wing the following month. No more operational postings followed and he returned to Poland in 1947 to continue his career with the post-war Polish Air Force, rising to the rank of General, despite a period of imprisonment between 1948 and 1956 due to his service with the RAF.

Personal mount of Wing Commander Skalski, Mustang III FZ152,coded 'SS'. He made his last two claims with this aircraft on 24 June 1944. *(via Chris Thomas)*

**SMIK,
Otto,
RAF**

RAF **No. 130678**

Slovak

DFC

Otto Smik was one of the very few Slovaks to become a fighter pilot in the RAF during the war. Born in the USSR, to a Slovak father and a Russian mother, Smik was too young to enlist in the pre-war Czechoslovakian Air Force before the country split off. While he could try his luck in the newly formed Air Force of Slovakia, recently independent, Smik, at the age of 17, chose to escape to France in March 1940 via Hungary. By June 1940 he had arrived in France but the country collapsed before he had the chance to be trained. Evacuated to the UK, he enlisted to the RAF in July. Trained in Canada, he returned in England as an officer in July 1942. Naturally posted to various Czech fighter squadrons from January 1943 onwards, he was not very welcome for various reasons and was eventually posted to No. 131 (County of Kent) Squadron, then in March to No. 122 (Bombay) Squadron where he made his first claim on the 13th (a probable Fw190). In May, another posting, No. 222 (Natal) Squadron, followed and it was here where he made most of his claims until October 1943 when his tour ended. He also received the DFC for his service during this tour.

In March 1944 he started a new tour of operations with No. 310 (Czechoslovakian) Squadron and it was with this unit that he made his last claims to bring his total to 10 confirmed victories (two shared), two probables, three damaged and three V-1s destroyed. In July he was posted to No. 312 (Czechoslovakian) Squadron as a Flight commander until being shot down on 3 September. He evaded capture and managed to return to the Allied lines at the end of October. The next month he was given command of **No. 127 Squadron**. However, on the 28th, he was shot down a second time, in Spitfire RR227, while leading a fighter-bomber operation over Holland.

A Spitfire LF.XVI of No. 127 Sqn (coded '9N') being serviced during the autumn of 1944. When Smik was shot down, the Mk.XVI had just been introduced into service with the 2 TAF and the mission he led that day was among the very first ones carried out by the mark.

Launce Smith joined the Auxiliary Air Force in 1932 and was among the first pilots to arrive at **No. 607 (County of Durham) Squadron**. In January 1939 he was given command of the squadron which was still equipped with Gladiators. When war broke out, the entire squadron was called to permanent duty and moved to France the following November.

When the Germans launched their offensive on 10 May 1940 607 had just transitioned to the Hurricane. Smith was on leave in Britain and he made a quick return to France but still missed the first two days of fighting. On 13 May he claimed a Bf109 destroyed. This was to be his only claim. Two days later, on 15 May, while leading a formation, made up of five aircraft from 607 and six from 615, providing escort to Blenheims, the fighters were caught by Bf109s and he was shot down and killed in his Hurricane (P2870).

View of Gloster Gladiators of No. 607 Sqn taken at Vitry-le-François in February 1940. The type was replaced before the German offensive.
(Andrew Thomas)

STEVENS,
Reginald Noel Basil, RAAF

AUS. 404672

Australian

DFC & Bar

A native of New South Wales, Australia, 'Reg' Stevens enlisted in the RAAF in January 1941 and was first posted as an NCO to No. 457 (RAAF) Squadron in the UK in December 1941. He volunteered to be sent to the Middle East in February 1942 and joined **No. 3 Squadron RAAF** in June, flying Kittyhawks. He opened his score on 27 October by shooting down an MC.202 and was commissioned the next month. Up to March 1943, other claims followed and he closed his score with two aircraft destroyed, one probable and two damaged and the position of flight commander, then OC in June. He was awarded the DFC in July. He left the squadron the next month to take command of **No. 451 (RAAF) Squadron** which had just seen its role change from an Army co-operation unit to a fighter one equipped with Spitfires. In December he relinquished command as he was at the end of his tour. In the meantime, in September, a Bar was added to his DFC. Repatriated to Australia, he served until the end of the war as a flying instructor at No. 2 OTU. He was discharged from the RAAF in July 1947.

Spitfire Mk.V EE792 was flown at the end of 1943 by S/L Stevens. It was during the last days of the Mk.V with this unit.

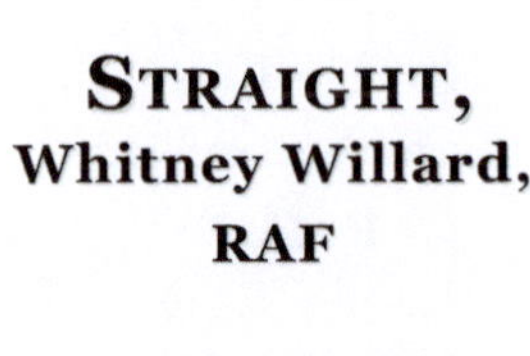

STRAIGHT,
Whitney Willard,
RAF

AAF **No. 90680**

British

DFC

American-born, Straight became a British subject in 1935. In 1939 he joined No. 601 (County of London) Squadron and was called up for full-time service at the end of August. He participated in the Norwegian campaign on ground duties but was injured during an air attack on 25 May 1940. He was evacuated and, upon recovery, returned to his former squadron at the end of September.

He made his first claim on 1 December and followed with another in February 1941. In April he was posted to **No. 242 (Canadian) Squadron** as OC with ground attack sorties being the main task. He made other claims during the following months to bring his total to four confirmed victories (one shared) and two probables (the last claim was recorded on 27 July). However, four days later, Straight, flying Hurricane Z2906, was shot down by light flak while attacking a destroyer off the coast of Normandy. A DFC was awarded in August.

While he was able to avoid capture by the Germans, he was interned by the Vichy French in the South of France until he escaped in June 1942. Reaching Gibraltar soon afterwards, he was back in England one month later. He spent the rest of the war in various positions in the Middle East and finished the war with the rank of Group Captain before being released a couple of months later.

In spring 1941 No. 242 Sqn was re-equipped with the Hurricane Mk.IIa. Z2588 had a short career and was lost in a crash-landing on 28 March.

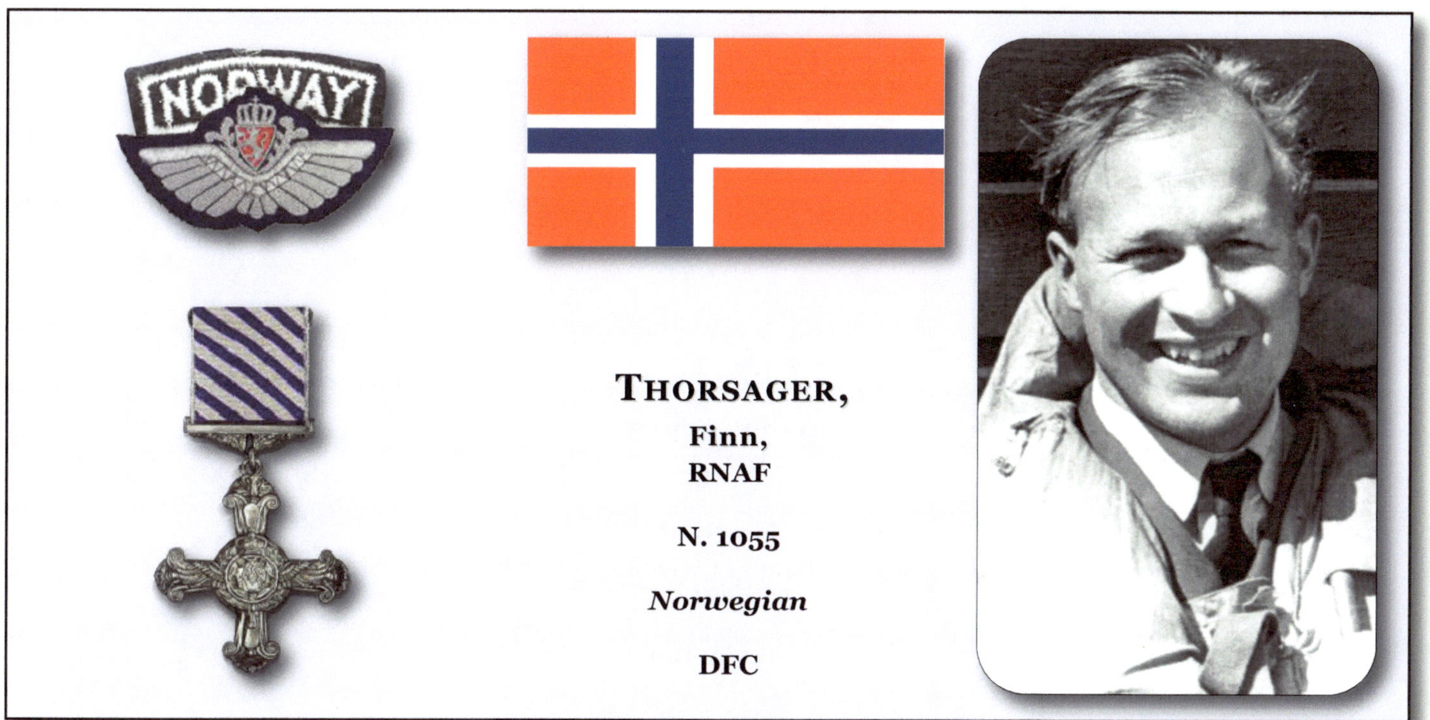

THORSAGER,
Finn,
RNAF

N. 1055

Norwegian

DFC

Finn Thorsager chose the career of a military pilot in 1936 when he joined the Norwegian Army Air Force. In April 1940, when the Germans invaded the country, Thorsager was a fighter pilot, flying Gladiators, based at Oslo. He became the first Norwegian pilot to fire at a German aircraft on 9 April.

He fled to Sweden in October 1940 and eventually reached Toronto in Canada in January 1941 where a Norwegian training base was located ('Little Norway'). After a refresher course, he stayed there as a flying instructor until June 1941 when he sailed for the UK. Upon his arrival he completed his training at an OTU and was then posted to No. 331 (Norwegian) Squadron in September. In March 1942 he was posted to the second Norwegian fighter squadron, **No. 332 (Norwegian) Squadron**, as a flight commander. During Operation 'Jubilee', over Dieppe, Thorsager managed to open his score by damaging two Fw190s. One year later, in February 1943, he was appointed to command the squadron and relinquished the role in July. During this period, other claims were added bringing his total to two confirmed victories (one shared) and seven damaged. A DFC followed in September.

He was not given any more operational appointments and ended the war in Ferry Command.

No. 332 (Norwegian) Sqn was formed in January on the Spitfire Mk.Va and became one of the very few units to have been entirely equipped with the rare mark. R7335 became Thorsager's regular mounts. This squadron was credited with more than 64 confirmed and probable victories, all on Spitfires. *(Finn Thorsager, via A. Thomas).*

UMBERS,
Arthur Ernest, RNZAF

NZ404003

New Zealander

DFC & Bar

'Spike' Umbers joined the RNZAF in November 1940. Trained in Canada, he sailed for the UK during the summer of 1941 and completed his course at No. 53 OTU. He was posted to No. 74 (Trinidad) Squadron in April 1941. In March 1942, when the second RZNAF fighter unit in Britain, No. 486 (NZ) Squadron, was formed, he was posted in. He did not open his score until December that year when he shared in a Do217 while flying his Typhoon. In September 1943, now a Flight commander, he was sent for a rest, having completed his tour, and was awarded the DFC. He returned to operations in April 1944 as a flight commander, flying Tempests, with No. 3 Squadron where he destroyed about 19 V-1s (three of which were shared) and received a Bar to his DFC (in July). In December 1944 he was again posted to **No. 486 (NZ) Squadron**, also flying Tempests, but this time as OC. He claimed three confirmed victories in January 1945 alone to bring his total to five confirmed victories (one shared), two probables (one shared), three aircraft damaged (one shared) and about 20 V-1s destroyed.

Sadly, on 14 February 1945, while conducting an armed reconnaissance over Germany, he was shot down by flak and killed in Tempest Mk. V NV715/SA-F.

No. 486 Sqn was one of the few units to have used the Tempest Mk. V on operations. This squadron saw considerable success with Tempest claiming 62 of its 87 confirmed or probable claims on the type. To this, we must also add close to 250 V-1s destroyed.
(Kalka family)

VAN DER STOK,
Bram,
RAF

RAF No. 106346

Dutch

-

'Bob' van der Stok was Dutch but from the Netherlands East Indies. He joined the Dutch Air Force in 1936 and when war hit the Netherlands he was a fighter pilot flying the Fokker D.XXI. On the first day of the invasion he managed to destroy a Bf109 and damage another. Sent back to civilian life, he formed a resistance cell and made three unsuccessful attempts to reach Great Britain. He finally succeeded and arrived in September 1941. Having been trained as a fighter pilot, his re-training was short and in February 1941 he was posted to No. 41 Squadron. In March and April 1942 he added a confirmed Bf109 and three damaged aircraft to his credit but his scoring was cut short on the 12th when he was shot down and became a PoW. In the following years he tried to escape many times and was eventually successful during the 'Great Escape' from Sagan in March 1944. While many of the escapers were later recaptured, and some executed, van der Stok was one of the three who were able to return to the UK. He finally made the 'home run' in July 1944. Following a refresher course, he was initially posted to No. 74 Squadron, in mid-February 1945 and was given command of **No. 322 (Dutch) Squadron** early in March 1945 and led this unit until the end of the war. In that time he completed about 20 sorties without adding to his tally. He left 322 in October that year.
After the war he emigrated to the USA.

Spitfire Mk.XVI TB997 of No. 322 Sqn, with a new canopy and coded 3W-V, seen in Germany shortly after the end of war. Bob van der Stok used to fly 3W-E.
(via Steve Brew - portrait)

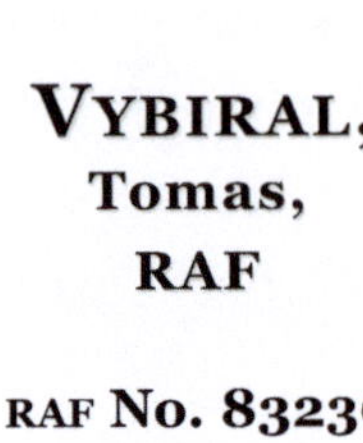

VYBIRAL,
Tomas,
RAF

RAF **No. 83236**

Czech

DSO, DFC

Tomas Vybiral was a pre-war Czechoslovakian Air Force pilot serving with Air Regiment 3. He escaped from his country in June 1939 and arrived in France soon afterwards where he enlisted in the Armée de l'Air. By May 1940 he was flying Curtiss H-75s with squadron GC I/5. During May and June 1940 he claimed seven confirmed victories (six shared). These were his only claims of the war. He retreated with his unit to North Africa and from there reached the United Kingdom via Gibraltar in August 1940. He was posted to

No. 312 (Czechoslovakian) Squadron at its foundation the same month after having been quickly retrained by the RAF. In June 1942 he completed his first tour but returned to 312 as a flight commander the following November for his second tour. He took command of the squadron on the first day of 1943 and kept this position until November when he was appointed WingCo flying of **No. 134 (Czechoslovakian) Wing** in March 1944 and remained at the head of the Wing until mid-November. He was awarded the DFC in July 1944 followed by the DSO in December. The DSO had originally been recommended as a Bar to his DFC but was changed by Air Marshal Roderic Hill. Vybiral returned to his country after the war but had to escape once more to Britain in September 1948 after the Communist coup in February.

The Spitfire Mk.IX, MK483/VY flown by Tomas Vybiral while at the head of No. 134 (Czech) Wing. Vybiral led the three Czechoslovakian squadrons during Operation *Overlord*. However, the wing was withdrawn at the end of June 1944.
(P. Vancata)

WARNES,
Geoffrey Berrington,
RAF

RAF No. 78429

British

DSO, DFC

Geoffrey Warnes joined the RAF in April 1940 and initially served in the Equipment Branch. In November he transferred to the General Duty Branch and underwent pilot training despite the unusual circumstance where his short sightedness forced him to wear contact lenses to fly.

In September 1941 he was posted to **No. 263 Squadron** upon the completion of his training. Flying Whirlwinds he became a flight commander in January 1942 and then, in December, took command of the squadron. In March 1943 he was awarded the DFC. He led 263 until the end of his tour in June 1943. The following month he became a DSO recipient and the only Whirlwind pilot to receive this decoration. In December that year he returned to 263 to lead once more for another tour of operations as the unit was about to convert to the Typhoon. On 22 February 1944, shortly after the squadron had been declared operational on the Typhoon, he had to ditch his aircraft, MN249, when returning from a shipping reconnaissance. He was seen swimming towards a dinghy but, despite an ASR operation being launched, he was posted missing.

P7043/HE-A in the autumn of 1942. This Whirlwind was one of the first to become a "Whirli-bomber" and was the mount of Flight Lieutenant G.B. Warnes.
(Jerry Brewer)

SQUADRONS!
No.3
Fighter Leaders
of the RAF, RAAF, RCAF, RNZAF & SAAF in WW2
Volume I
Phil H. Listemann
Fighter Leaders
RAAF, RCAF, RNZAF & SAAF in WW2
Volume III
Phil H. Listemann
USN AIRCRAFT 1922-1962
G-228
Vol.4:
Type Designation Letters
'BF', 'BT' & 'F' (Pt-1)
RAF, Dominion & Allied Squadron
at War:
Study, History and Statistics
No.137 Squadron
1941 - 1945
Compiled by
Phil H. Listemann
with
Chris Thomas
SQUADRONS!
No.10
The North American
Mustang Mk. IV
in Western Europe
www.RAF-IN-COMBAT.com
- USN Aircraft 1922-1962 -
- Squadrons! -
- RAF, Dominion and Allied squadrons at War -
- Allied Wings -
- Famous squadrons of WW2 -
- Fighter Leaders -
RAF, Dominion & Allied Squadron
at War:
Study, History and Statistics
No.131 (County of Kent) Squadron
1941 - 1945
Famous Commonwealth Squadrons of WW2
No.453 (R.A.A.F.) Squadron
1941-1945
Buffalo, Spitfire
ALLIED WINGS
ALLIED WINGS